CHINA AND CAPITALISM

T0083589

Understanding China:
New Viewpoints on History and Culture

Each book in **Understanding China** series provides a short and accessible guide to the research highlights of an active field of Chinese studies. Focusing on interdisciplinary work that bridges the humanities and social sciences, the books introduce readers to the subject, discuss the major problems and, by critically analyzing competing solutions and taking up new viewpoints, draw readers into the debates. The books are written in language accessible to readers outside Chinese studies, but are sufficiently informative, current and provocative also to engage the specialist reader.

Editors: David Faure, The Chinese University of Hong Kong and University of Oxford

Helen F. Siu, Yale University and the Hong Kong Institute of Humanities and Social Sciences

CHINA AND CAPITALISM

A History of Business Enterprise in Modern China

David Faure

香港大學出版社
HONG KONG UNIVERSITY PRESS

Hong Kong University Press
14/F Hing Wai Centre
7 Tin Wan Praya Road
Aberdeen
Hong Kong

© Hong Kong University Press 2006

ISBN 962 209 783 9 (Hardback)
ISBN 962 209 784 7 (Paperback)

Secure On-line Ordering
http://www.hkupress.org

British Library Cataloguing-in-Publication Data
A catalogue record for this book is available from the British Library.

Printed and bound by Kings Time Printing Press Ltd., in Hong Kong, China

Contents

Acknowledgements

The substance of this book came from lectures I gave over the years in my own classes and at conferences. Among the many people to thank, therefore, are my students in the Economic History of Modern China course which I gave in the 1980s, who were much confused by my stubborn reluctance to accept the standard published wisdoms of the day which was only matched by my inability to come up with an alternative. However, I must thank Professors Hsu Hung and Choi Chi-cheung for providing the occasion in 1993 to make me summarize my ideas for a series of lectures at the Hong Kong University of Science and Technology (HKUST). Comments also came from readers of the booklet that was produced by the Division of Humanities at HKUST from those lectures. Professor Raj Brown included Chapter 4 into her, ed. *Chinese Business Enterprise, First Edition*, London: Routledge, 1996, Vol. 4 and I thank her for comments on that and on the other chapters. I am grateful to Professors Helen Siu, Choi Chi-cheung, Lai Chi-kong, and Dr Cyril Lin, for commenting on the early draft, and Dr Ho Hon-wai for correcting some of my gross blunders.

David Faure

1 Introduction

Towards the end of 1978 when the Chinese leadership decided to re-open the country to foreign trade and investment, the implications of the policy turn-around were neither as clearly set out nor necessarily as destined to succeed as it is sometimes now thought. Yet, overnight, it became clearly established that the aspiration towards modernization was to be fostered through China's taking its part in the international economy. Overnight, a generation in the writing of Chinese history was overthrown: gone was the foreign impact as a decided detriment on China's fortune and in its place was capital investment as a contribution to economic growth. Through the 1980s, social and economic historians writing within the People's Republic of China and accustomed to thinking about Chinese history in relation to capitalist oppression had had to grope for a new way forward, and that began a long process of rethinking China's history.

I shall not summarize the literature which went into this tortuous process. Readers who are interested in the outcome can read Xu Dixin and Wu Chengming's three volumes on the history of capitalism in China, or, for another strand in the argument, turn to the writings of Ma Min and Zhu Ying which deal with the shift in the Qing state's perception and treatment of merchants in the spate of reforms begun in the early years of the twentieth century.[1] The one line of thought traces the history of the market in China, and the other addresses the question of the rise of "civil society". The history of the market and the position of merchants are fundamental in understanding the history of Chinese business and these works in the 1980s may be cited as examples which cleared the ground for further research.

In the meantime, China's increasing importance in the world economy and a growing interest in incorporating China into world history has brought about a demand for generalizations about Chinese economic and social history. In my view, China historians — writing from within or outside China — are ill prepared to satisfy the demand. A few exceptions to the contrary, since the 1950s, little interest has been shown in examining China's historical statistics in any systematic manner; few studies have looked at the structures of Chinese business corporations, and hardly any China historian has examined the history of technology in the nineteenth and twentieth centuries.[2] Despite the pioneering effort on the history of accounting produced by two Chinese historians, the significance of that subject is poorly grasped.[3] Contemporary documents are always in short supply, but not even when they are abundant has research conducted been published, or, more often, been conducted at all. Moreover, a great deal of what is published is still available only in Chinese and remains inaccessible to most Western historians who are not also China specialists. A greater gulf exists between the China historian (whether or not ethnic Chinese) and his or her Western counterpart who is interested in drawing China into world history, than between the Chinese historian of the 1990s and earlier decades.

Language is such an obvious barrier in writing history that any warning for the non-Chinese reader in wrestling with Chinese history seems superfluous. However, it is necessary to point out the lack of critical analysis in a great deal that is written about China in the general vein. It is useful to be reminded of the saying "easy comes, easy goes", which applies to quick scholarship as it does to home finance. It sounds very old-fashioned nowadays to say that historians should learn to read the footnotes. When the footnotes refer to documents in languages which the reader cannot understand, it may be obvious but it needs pointing out that it is very easy for writers to take liberty with the documentation, and some do.

The only answer to shoddy documentation is, of course, more and more careful research. Yet, in republishing this small volume, I think it is worth presenting this history of Chinese business in outline even at this stage because I think in my short lectures of 1993, I presented a view of Chinese history which, even now, goes somewhat against the grain of present scholarship. To my mind, the current discussion has, probably as a result of over-correction to charges of "orientalism", underscored China's cultural differences from the West. The Western-centred post-industrial world is too full of the importance of individual rights and liberties to appreciate the workings of a society ruled more by ritual than by law. In saying this, I am not defending the penchant for characterizing Chinese business by imputing to it strong affinities for "guanxi" (read "connections") or "face". I find these crude characterizations quite misleading as tools for understanding Chinese society. At heart, I think the ritual, rather than legal, definition of interpersonal relationships in business relates to the manner of incorporation, and that, in turn, is closely tied up with the control of property.

Let me state briefly my argument in this book. When the capital market in the fifteenth century did not take off, Chinese business advanced through patronage and incorporation facilitated by ritual (rather than law). The transformation of this structure came about under the Western impact in the second half of the nineteenth century. It had taken China all of the twentieth century to make the transformation and to this day, it is far from complete.

To put this brief outline into context, it can be said that business practices in China had been shaped by the broader trends in the evolution of the Chinese state and society since 1500. To take the long view, it is necessary to recognize that three changes, in particular, provided for the backbone of long-lasting development in the late imperial state of the Ming (1368–1644) and the Qing (1644–1911) dynasties. Firstly, the economy was increasingly monetarized from the sixteenth century as silver was imported into China in large quantities from abroad (in return for Chinese exports). Secondly, the recruitment of a bureaucracy by examination, long instituted since the Tang dynasty, was consistently applied without any break from the early Ming into the last years of the Qing dynasty, and, whether or not the content of the examination shaped an efficient government, it created a class of administrators who prided themselves on their scholarship. The same sense of pride became a basis for lineage organization in the richer parts of China which produced more than the average number of examination degree holders. Thirdly, the scholar-official class, from the 1500s, saw their political interests vested in the maintenance of ritual order which assigned all members of the state, including the emperor, rights and responsibilities. It is possible to read into this development the political agenda long raised by Neo-Confucians in the Song dynasty, but it was only from the sixteenth century, after various crises shattered the hold the emperor might have had on court officials, and a scholar-official class grew in number and wealth over many parts of the realm, that the scholar officialdom achieved the unity of purpose as a political force. In the background, it is important to draw attention to the vast size of the Chinese state even in 1500. When the emperor ruled over a population of 100 million, no officialdom was capable of enforcing the emperor's order except through the connivance of the local elite, which itself aspired to official status. Stability was maintained in late imperial China not by strict enforcement of law but by connivance between the officialdom and the local leadership to maintain the propriety of rituals.[4]

In Chapters 1 to 3 I shall describe how business was conducted under the late imperial regime. I shall argue that in the sixteenth century, with the exception of the salt trade, run as a government monopoly but in which merchant capital was drawn through a market in futures, Chinese business was conducted by merchants who, most of the time, were unregulated, and who transacted with one another with little resort to the law. As an aside, I shall also look briefly at the history of Chinese technology, especially with the view of coming to an understanding as to why it was so difficult for China to adopt steam technology in the nineteenth century, the answer for which question rested on the lack of a machine tool industry. This much should be common knowledge to the field. However, this characterization of Chinese business omits the very important need of incorporation. In other words, surely enough, Chinese people contracted, but when they did not contract as individuals, how did they do it? The answer I present in Chapter 3 argues that they did so as lineages, a term used in the literature on China to refer to groups of people tracing common descent rather than the lines of descent themselves. Relationships in the lineage group were regulated more by ritual and patronage than by law, and for that reason, ritual and patronage had a strong place in Chinese business institutions.

From the end of the nineteenth century into the first half of the twentieth century, incorporation through ritual practices came to be challenged by practices introduced through Western law. That did not happen overnight, nor did it imply the immediate disappearance of the ritual corporations. Instead, in this period which went astride the end of the Chinese empire and the establishment of the Chinese Republic, rituals which were established in the late imperial period were increasingly pitched against what seemed Western and modern. A century-long process began whereby incorporation on the ritual basis had to be replaced by incorporation resting on the strength of law. Chapter 4 outlines the beginnings of the process in relation to the introduction of Company Law in China from the late nineteenth century (enacted in the British colony of Hong Kong in 1865 and in China by 1904), and Chapter 5 the resumption of the process from the last years of the 1970s after a break of four decades.

In the background, it is necessary to appreciate the momentous changes which came over Chinese society as the Qing empire drew to a close. The last word has not been said about the Revolution of 1911 which overthrew monarchy in China. Nevertheless, we know enough about it as historians to realize that it did not come about only because the government was inept and Westernized young people brought it about through their revolutionary parties.[5] The government was inept and seen to be so because it was defeated in war, first in 1840 to Britain (in the Opium War), and then, in 1895, to Japan (the Sino-Japanese War), and it could not deal with the inflation of the early 1900s which it had created by debasing the coinage. Some time in between those events, the central government in Beijing had come to financial ruins. The Taiping Rebellion in the 1850s and 1860s had undercut its ability to raise revenue from the land tax which it had depended on through the eighteenth century, and, so, through the last decades of the nineteenth century, but especially after 1895, it was increasingly burdened by war indemnity and financial calls for military reforms. The inability of government to deliver cast doubt on the very ideology on which it had commanded respect in earlier centuries. The same scholarly tradition which had held the Chinese state together in the eighteenth century, by the end of the nineteenth century, appeared backward. By 1900, even the imperial court had accepted the need for a complete overhaul, and it was that effort which brought down the government.

There was, of course, a technological gap between China and its invading powers, but China's inability to fill it had to do with the weaknesses of its social institutions in mobilizing resources. Some of these weaknesses could justifiably be attributed to conservatism. The scholars who looked upon the imperial examination as their preserve were hardly likely to look favourably at a new syllabus to be adopted from the West over which they had no expertise. However, many more weaknesses had to do with the lack of a commercial tradition rooted in law. Until Western law came to be applied in China – more of that in Chapter 4 — China did not have any law which dealt with the business company. When the imperial government launched into railway building, therefore, and permitted the provinces to raise capital for it through joint-stock operations, the mechanisms were not present to hold the company promoters accountable to shareholders. In inland Sichuan province, the railway company went bankrupt before the railway was built, and shareholders were aggrieved to find the central government demanding the railway nationalized without providing for compensation. Multiply such confusion manifold as government abolished the imperial examinations, increased tax, founded new schools, instituted police forces, and implemented many more new policies, all at a time the debased coinage was fostering inflation in the market place, and one can understand why it was so popularly thought by 1908 that the imperial government was inept. When in 1911, a portion of the army stationed in Wuchang revolted, the government found it had to deal with not only that localized incident, but a crisis of confidence that was widely felt throughout the country.

The Republican government which was formed in the wake of the success of revolution in 1911 did not ever have the chance to succeed. Implementing a constitutional government by popular election in 1912 was too drastic a change to comprehend for any but a tiny fraction of China's newly educated elite. The central government, which was ruined financially before then, depended on foreign loans to survive, and, so, secret negotiations for loans which were to benefit only the parties involved in negotiation eroded any further confidence in government. Power devolved very soon to military commanders, dubbed "warlords" by their opponents, while the country fragmented. Significantly, political fragmentation was not accompanied by economic disaster. Despite continual wars between army factions, for reasons that will be given in Chapter 4, which had to do with the devolution of political patronage of business, the economy boomed from 1900 to the early 1930s. A nascent working class coming from the mines, the railways and new-found urban industries, gave enough of a hint that the new industrialization might be the course for further revolution to enable the Comintern to foster revolutionary cells in China. One of these was the Chinese Communist Party, which was to be fostered within the Guomindang Party which the Comintern also had a strong hand in re-organizing. It will be too much of a detour in this account to describe the very important transformation of Chinese politics introduced by these two parties. Suffice it to say that when the Guomindang Party defeated the northern warlords and set up a government in Nanjing in 1927, it re-established the authority of a centralized regime. Its decade of rule from Nanjing, a nightmare scenario for any government, fraught with internal and external wars, depression and considerable internal dissension, saw the beginnings of a government policy which was increasingly concerned with centralizing its control on the economy. War with Japan came in 1937, followed by civil war between the Guomindang Party and the Chinese Communist Party from 1945 to 1949. Effective centralized government was re-established only in the People's Republic in 1949.[6]

Between 1949 and 1978, despite the occasional shifts in policy — which were real and consequential — it may be said that the economy was increasingly put under a command regime. Central planning, however, did not ever produce the plans which allowed effective central control, and by the Cultural Revolution, which broke out in 1966, the planners themselves were no longer in place, let alone the plan. The very marked features of the Chinese economy, therefore, were not produced by planning, but by some very drastic measures which put enormous strain on the central government for driving the economy. Inheriting runaway inflation and substantial debts from the previous government, the People's Republic in 1949 moved towards closing the economy to the outside world, effectively by abrogating foreign debts, introducing strict exchange controls, rationing and restricting the movement of its people abroad. For three decades, increasing radicalization of political and economic policies totally squeezed out the market. By the Great Leap Forward in 1959, no private enterprise was in operation in China and practically all farmland was held by communes, and by the Cultural Revolution beginning in 1966, even accounting was regarded as a bouregoise indulgence and suspended in many state and communal enterprises. The net result was an initial spurt in heavy industry in the 1950s and a stagnant economy thereafter. Economic policy took an about turn towards the end of 1978, when in recognition of the need for both political and economic reform, the Chinese government took the bold step of requiring the communes to contract land out to farmers, permitting individual business enterprises — at first on a small scale, but the scale of operation grew very rapidly — and promoting foreign investment in coastal cities designated as "special economic zones". Back in 1978, no-one foresaw the extent to which privatization might go. Throughout the 1980s, the opening of the Chinese economy to world trade and investment was called into question with every political upheaval. However, by the 1990s, it was widely recognized that economic opening had become irreversible.[7]

The process whereby law overtook ritual as the foundation of business took most of the twentieth century and to this day, the process is far from complete. That should be no surprise. After all, it took ritual three centuries (from the sixteenth to the eighteenth century) to be firmly established as the fundamental political principle whereby society might be held together. A great deal more historical research is needed to flesh out in full the implications of this argument, but there is enough, on the basis of published research, to shape a general outline. In the long term, we are probably only now, in the early years of the twenty-first century, able to perceive in broad outline the new China that was taking shape. Business behaviour which rested on ritual and patronage differs in significant ways from that regulated by law, and in Chapter 6, the concluding chapter, I ponder on what these differences might be.

2 The Sprouts of Capitalism

Every now and then, it becomes an issue among historians what endemic features in Chinese society had held back the country's economic development in the nineteenth century. In the latest round, they have been driven to focus their minds, by Andre Gunther Frank, on the impact made on late imperial China by the inflow of silver, and by Kenneth Pomeranz, on institutional and technological similarities between Europe and China. Eighteenth-century China was wealthy, technologically sound, highly literate by pre-modern standards and adept in business.[1] Why should China not have undergone the coal-and-iron industrial transformation of the nineteenth century as smoothly as did Europe and America?

We can begin in common agreement that the silver inflow into China from the sixteenth century to the eighteenth century brought about a commercial revolution. China was then the world's powerhouse, and silver was brought to China as Chinese products were exported abroad. The exports included silk and porcelain, produced at technological standards unmatched in the West. They included also tea, consumed in ever larger quantities in Britain, satisfying not only the new fads of consumption but also, through import duties, the royal coffers.[2] Yet, China's trade in the eighteenth century consisted of much more than what was exported. Visitors to China at the time noted the abundance created by its internal trade, the high productivity of its rural population, its magnificent cities and, despite the low rates of taxes, the vast resources of the imperial government. To eighteenth-century Europe, China was a model of the rational society, where the emperor ruled through a scholarly class recruited by examination and the common people knew their place.[3]

Nevertheless, China did not go on to build the steam engine, or create the investment environment which might smooth the way for the introduction of nineteenth-century industry. To stress the similarities between China's experience and Europe's is to gloss over essential features in the emergence of the industrial West. To recap those essentials very briefly, it may be said that while it is true that commercial institutions which evolved in China brought unprecedented economic growth from the sixteenth century to the eighteenth century, the same institutions were inadequate for handling the scale of operations needed in the nineteenth-century world of steam-driven enterprises, namely the factory, the railway and the steamer. Nineteenth-century development called for the investment of capital on a scale hitherto unknown, not only to China, but also to the West. The West had been able to cope because the foundations for industrial banking, incorporation and commercial law had been laid in the sixteenth century. They made possible the creation of credit instruments which could be traded on a financial market, and which financed trade and industry. Financial instruments, indeed, also appeared in China in the sixteenth century. But the financial market in China never took off, and, as a result, China did not find it easy to develop its own banks, paper money, shares or bonds. In short, whether or not China had the capital for steam-driven technology, aside from the government itself, China did not possess the mechanism for focusing enough of it on industrial enterprises. It might well be true, as Pomeranz would claim, that the divergence of industrial strength between the West and China became apparent only by the nineteenth century, but that is not to say that the reasons for the emergence of that divergence are not to be located in a much earlier age.

In this book, I discuss these issues in the context of China's historical encounter with capitalism. The word "capitalism", with ideological and historicist overtones, is necessarily nebulous. Chinese historians have often used it to refer to a stage in historical development and that is not the sense in which I use the word. I use it in relation to its roots in the concept of "capital", a component of wealth as posited by the classical economists. In this book, in considering China's encounter with capitalism, I want to consider the history of the application of the institutions which enabled capital to impact on the economy. It is in this sense that this book is meant to be an institutional study, a study of the institutions of capitalism. It is in relation to the institutions of capitalism that I shall explain how China diverged from the West, why the Chinese economy was so successful in the eighteenth century and why it suffered so greatly in the nineteenth and twentieth centuries.

Let me begin by stating my basic standpoint in relation to the China history literature. In classical economics, "capital" was a component of wealth that was distinguishable from land and labour, just as interest as a price component would have been distinguishable from rent and wage. What made capital different from labour was that it might be accumulated, and what made it different from land was that it was readily transferable.[4] Classical economics did not ask what it was that made it possible for capital to circulate. It merely assumed that capital was created in the process of exchange, of which trade was a major component, and that trade itself was part of the order of nature, accompanying the division of labour. A history of the market, therefore, came to be written only when this point of view was challenged in the early years of the twentieth century, by Max Weber and Karl Polanyi, whose views of the development of capitalist institutions strongly characterize my own reading of Chinese history. Weber and Polanyi suggested that contrary to the classical economist's assumption, unequal advantages did not naturally lead to trade, for trade could only proceed when the institutions for it had been created. By institutions they referred to arrangements for the settlement of obligations such as money, especially paper money, accounting, law and as Karl Marx himself would have recognized, banks. Ferdnand Braudel has since reconstructed the outline history of many of these institutions. China had, once again, fallen behind, because China historians have not been equal to their Western counterparts in elucidating these mechanisms in the historical Chinese economy.[5]

A focus on the history of capitalism in China, therefore, does not rest on an account of China's economic prosperity but on the evolution of capitalist instruments. The mechanisms for capitalism have to be instruments for the holding and circulation of capital, that is to say, money, and frequently, paper instruments including land deeds, account books, contracts, shares, bonds and any certificate of savings or loans of any sort, and the institutions that serviced them, be they family firms, chartered companies, temples or lineages.[6] It is not sufficient to state, as many studies of the China scene do, that "merchants" were involved in agriculture or industry; it matters *how* they were involved. And it is not sufficient to argue that China had been dominated by an ideology which relegated trade to second place; it matters a great deal more *how*, despite the denigration of the merchant, trading could have been so successful in imperial China, and agriculture and industry in some parts of China could have achieved high enough a standard of technological excellence at competitive costs to win the very substantial markets both within China and overseas. It must not be assumed that the mechanisms which made it possible for merchants to engage in the economy necessarily employed many instruments for the circulation or preservation of capital, or that the instruments were necessarily very efficiently employed. The employment of such instruments had much to do with beliefs and social practices, the law and its enforcement, and political patronage.

Let it be said at the outset that China did not have to face the ideological hurdle against lending money at interest which was imposed by religion in the West. The Daoist manual, the *Taishang ganying bian*, begins with a story of profit awarded by the gods from speculation in the sale of medicine at a time of epidemic in return for devoted recitation of the religious literature. Moreover, despite the frequent reference to the denigration of trade in the secondary literature, Chinese officials had no difficulty allowing for trade, having long realized that for the sake of the material welfare of the state, trade was needed "so that areas that had might exchange with areas that did not have". If agriculture had to be given precedence before trade, and investment in land was set apart from other sorts of investment as if neither profit nor management was expected, it was because the dominant economic view was physiocratic. The idea that the market might be independent of the state came late to China, as it did to the West. Yet, the phyisocratic world-view did not fall short of expositions on the craft of government. Without reaching back across the millennia for an origin, we can still point to a vast literature accumulated on "statecraft" from the sixteenth to the eighteenth century. Embodied in it are blueprints on the management of resources, ranging from mines to rivers, household registration, the minting of coins, the desirability of fixing prices, the requirements of a civil service, the ideals and practices of taxation, the provision of granaries and famine relief, and many more subjects with implications on the economy. As the imperial government became more sophisticated in the craft of government from the sixteenth to the eighteenth century, its knowledge of the country's geography and regional customs, legal or illegal, expanded by leaps and bounds. The details of knowledge woven into government practices go far beyond any simple statement about the Confucian ideology might indicate.[7]

This is why, even in the physiocratic context, it may be said that by the 1820s, Chinese economic thinking was quickly discovering the market. One consequence of this discovery was the belief in bullionism that eventually led to the Opium War.[8] Soon after that war, in 1853, when the Xianfeng emperor was set on debasing the coinage, his minister Wang Maoyin memorialized the throne to warn that although the government had the power and the means to devalue the coinage, it did not have the same power and means to prevent the people from raising prices. Marx came to the same conclusion in the chapter in *Capital* in which Wang was cited in a footnote. However, such occasional demonstration of an awareness of the independence of the market by a minority of officials did not overturn the anti-commercial stance of the imperial government, that had denied the necessity of opening China to overseas trade and downgraded mercantile activities. Wang was castigated by the imperial court for suggesting that paper notes should be fully convertible, a view that seemed to the court to defend the merchant's interest but not the state's.[9] Without knowing it, Marx reflected the changing mood about China in the nineteenth-century West. After years of exertion to counter restrictions imposed on their trade, Western merchants in China, confined to the southern port of Guangzhou (known for long as Canton), had been publicizing the imperial government's anti-merchant and anti-trade inclinations. Subject to a law which stressed collective rather than individual responsibilities, and private connections and interpersonal settlements in money or gift rather than strict terms of law, Western merchants had come to the view that the imperial government was as inept as its officials and their underlings were corrupt. China's losing the Opium Wars in 1841–42 and 1858–60 confirmed that the country was militarily weak and socially restless. When efforts to acquire the new industries had failed in the second half of the nineteenth century, an imperial government which refused to see the economy from the merchant's point of view could readily be blamed for China's supposed backwardness.[10]

However, it would not really be correct to ascribe China's economic backwardness to the ineffectiveness of its government. In the long run, the government's administrative effectiveness went through its ups and downs. Compared to the unwieldiness of the Ming government up to the seventeenth century, the Qing government was a model of bureaucratic efficiency. Although it responded in an ad hoc manner to the foreign threat of the nineteenth century, it was authoritative and efficient in its internal administration through most of the eighteenth.[11] In the eighteenth century, it was successful in raising tax revenue, its economic policies were effective, and its officials had a better understanding of the nation's economy than their successors in the second half of the nineteenth century. And, during the eighteenth century, the Chinese economy boomed, driven, not by government programmes, but by the market. Any explanation of nineteenth-century backwardness, therefore, cannot rest on the belief that it was in the nature of the imperial Chinese government to be opposed to trade, but must resort instead, as Chinese historians do, to the combination of weaknesses in Chinese business institutions *and* the inability of the government to rectify them. Taking into account the wealth of the Chinese empire that so impressed Westerners in the eighteenth century as well as China's failure to industrialize in the nineteenth, therefore, Chinese historians have long referred to the three centuries from the sixteenth century to the eighteenth as the period of the "sprouts of capitalism". The use of the term recognizes that even though the institutions that eventually made capitalism a reality in the West also appeared in China in the Ming and the Qing, they did not, as in the West, grow into fruition. [12] Dipping into this history written by Chinese historians in the twentieth century, one finds references in plenty to the emergence of commercial institutions on the one hand, and their stagnation on the other. Yet, as I have indicated, the literature is fraught with difficulties, for it has looked for capitalism in the wrong places.

Capitalism, in fact, did sprout in the sixteenth century, promoted by the Ming dynasty government. It was destroyed also by the government in the seventeenth century. This is evident in the history of the salt trade.

To look for the sprouts of capitalism in the sixteenth-century salt trade, it will be necessary first to counter the argument of Chinese historians who think they have found it in the wage labour embedded in the booming handicraft industries. It is true that Ming dynasty workshop owners hired labourers, but to argue that this fact in itself implied the existence of capitalism is to leave out of the picture the essential linkage of the classical economist's formula which is at the heart of Marx's description of capitalism, particularly, the question of how capital circulated in the context of the workshop. If the existence of wage labour was all it took to create incipient capitalism, we should not wonder that some historians have found it all the way from ancient China.[13] The historical problem should then not be if incipient capitalism had sprouted in China, but why, if the institution had remained static for two millennia, it might not continue to do so for much longer.

The argument that searches for incipient capitalism in the workshop of the Ming and the Qing mistakes the workshop for the factory. The handicraft workshop was neither a capitalist institution nor set upon a course that might turn it into one. The factory was, but it was a creation of the Western Industrial Revolution in the first half of the nineteenth century, and it involved, as much as the use of hired labour which one also finds in the workshop, the application of accounting methods for the control of production that was quite absent in Chinese workshop production.[14] Chinese labour management in the workshop and elsewhere did not provide the means for the direct hiring of large numbers of workmen. In the cases that can be documented, although the Chinese had been very successful in conducting labour-intensive projects employing large numbers of workers under administrative command, no attempt to run a business enterprise on any comparable scale ever succeeded. The Chinese imperial workshops for the production of silk were conceived on the grand scale — they were planned on the basis that they would include several hundred looms each — but were for hardly any time managed as unified enterprises. Instead, business operations took the form that observers for many years in Hong Kong and now in south China are familiar with, for the imperial factory was not managed centrally, but contracted out to skilled master workmen, who ran their own independent enterprises using only one or two looms each.[15] Similar processes of managerial fragmentation may be documented for the mines and the imperial kilns. Mine shafts and kilns were individually owned, and contracted out to small teams of workmen working under their own headmen.[16] At the imperial mint, government retained ownership of the machinery, but headmen hired their own workmen.[17] One suspects that without some form of production accounting, supervision costs would have been high, and it would have been cheaper to sub-contract than to hire.

The corollary of this is that when the factory appeared in China, China took to factory management with the minimum of difficulty. Until the 1920s, Chinese factory owners managed their workforces through contractors, who recruited, supervised, paid them and received a lump sum payment for the effort. The modern factory did house many workers in the same compound, but management continued largely in traditional decentralized lines. What had happened probably came about not so much as a conscious change in managerial thinking as the subtle adaptation of traditional practice to preconditions imposed by newly introduced machinery. The power loom, the cigarette roller, and the cement works, products of the Industrial Revolution, could make use of unskilled labour to replace the skilled labour that was needed in the traditional workshop. It was not until the 1920s, in their effort to rationalize, that Chinese factory managers began to replace traditional contractors with employed supervisors, a process that created a considerable amount of industrial dispute and which drove the contractors onto the side of their labourers as industrial action spread.[18] The argument that links the workshop to the factory, therefore, ignores the vitality of the new discipline associated with the use of power machinery, which, incidentally, is fundamental to Marx's insightful discussion on the industrial worker's alienation from his work.

Just as in Europe, there was little in the way of capitalist institutions in the running of the workshop. Instead, the source for capitalist practices has to be found in the history of incorporation as a practice, in trade, in the ownership of land and in finance. If capitalism had indeed sprouted in the Ming and the Qing, surely, what needs explaining is why it was that the growth of native financial institutions was so thwarted that the capitalists who might provide large industrial loans did not emerge from the native Chinese context before the Western banks were able to lend substantially to China. It has a lot to do with the instruments for the storage and transfer of capital, the history of which we find in the history of the salt trade.

In the background, it must be noted, Ming and the Qing businesses were owned by families, as they were in Europe until the twentieth century. No less than their counterparts in sixteenth-century England, Chinese merchants depended on social networks built around patron-client relationships. However, some time in the seventeenth century, the situation changed rather dramatically in the West, particularly in England. Private ownership of property was given a place of political importance, patronage networks directed by the royal household and its retainers fell apart, and the money men, as money men, began to play a prominent role in politics. The most dramatic of all this development came in the course of events that led from the formation of the chartered companies to the founding of the Bank of England in 1694, with somewhere in between, the rise of the London stock exchange.[19] Chinese merchants, as merchants, did not have a stake in politics. Chinese cities were, as Max Weber pointed out, seats of government. What Weber had not realized was that Chinese towns were, indeed, run by merchants, who masqueraded as scholar officials.[20] In China, the economic growth of the sixteenth century led on to another course of development: individualism never gained a political foothold, merchants did not form an estate, and it was the idea of collective responsibility in the form of the ancestral lineage that came to mediate between the individual and the state.[21] Merchants sought protection from the state via the lineage's private connections within the bureaucracy. Political patronage became so common from high to low in society that it was sought not only from officials but also from eunuchs and from the imperial family. Hence, the stories of corruption, of the exchanges of favours between those with money and those with power.[22]

Following Braudel, we may also note that mercantile activities in the Ming and Qing were structured in tiers. There were, for instance, the hawkers of the rural markets, that remarkable institution that had been made possible by unshakable faith in the independence of silver as a standard of value. There were the merchants that serviced the markets, the brokers that sought out opportunities, the middlemen that purchased and sold, the contractors and the many dealers on whom Arthur Smith and Fei Hsiao-tung have left us such vivid descriptions and that G. William Skinner skilfully sewed into a marketing network spanning villages and provincial capitals.[23] Beyond the rural markets, the sleepy county cities, and even, perhaps, many a prefectural seat, there was the world of high finance, dominated for centuries by the Huizhou merchants, known in particular for their capital in the pawnshop business, the Yangzhou salt merchants, probably half of whom were of Huizhou origin, the Shanxi merchants, who in the late eighteenth and nineteenth centuries came to be known for the remittance networks, and then, of course, in the same period, the merchant households of Guangzhou known to Westerners as the Cohong.[24] The imperial family itself, as we now know, was not above business undertakings. Trusted servants of the emperor, such as the households described in the famous novel, the

Dream of the Red Chamber, invested their wealth in pawnshops.[25] It is also well documented that by the eighteenth century, it was common practice for county governments to bank their reserves with merchants in return for an interest.[26] The practice continued into the twentieth century: in the famous case of the collapse of the rubber market in 1910, the Shanghai *daotai,* the most senior Chinese official in Shanghai, almost went bankrupt for having invested the city's reserves in local banks that had become insolvent as rubber shares collapsed.[27]

In this hierarchy of interlocking commercial and financial relationships, patronage from the top filtered all the way to the very bottom. For this reason, it may be argued that where China diverged from Europe, it was because government had stifled high finance. The stifling of high finance can be discerned in the history of the Huizhou merchants. We do not know nearly enough about them. About these financiers: a popular saying in the Qing had it that a place in which the Huizhou merchants did not do business might not be considered a market. They worked closely within their own networks, often among kinsmen and fellow villagers. They operated partnerships, drawing capital from working and sleeping partners alike. In the bigger cities, they had their own guilds, and observed a status order that was well regulated. Besides their involvement in the salt trade, they also ran pawnshops, not singly, but in chains, the bigger pawnshops lending to the smaller ones. The wealthiest Huizhou merchants lived in Yangzhou, the centre of the salt trade, and supported the artists for which Yangzhou came to be famous. However, they also maintained lineages back home in Huizhou, and it was back to Huizhou that quite a few, apparently, had their bodies sent for burial even when they had spent their entire working lives away. Like other wealthy households of the Ming and the Qing, their sons sat the imperial examinations, and many of them obtained official titles. Wealthy Huizhou lineages occupied high places on the Ming and Qing social hierarchy.[28]

The Huizhou merchants became wealthy in the first instance from the salt trade in the Ming. They probably transported salt as well, but many were involved in the futures market. The market in salt futures arose when in the early Ming (late fifteenth century), the emperor needed to have grain transported to the troops that garrisoned the northern border but did not have the means to do so except by mortgaging his monopoly on the production and transport of salt. The arrangement for this was quite complex. The merchant who intended to deal in salt would first have to perform for the government the service of transporting a quantity of grain to the garrisons. Upon delivery of the grain, he was given a receipt, which he could then produce in Nanjing in exchange for the certificate bearing his entitlement of salt. Because the salt trade was managed as a government monopoly, tight regulations specified where he might then purchase and sell his salt allotment. If all this arrangement sounds clumsy, it must be remembered that status registration was still enforced in the early Ming, that taxation was not unified and that the government operated on the principle that specific services might be demanded from registered households in addition to tax payment in kind as well as money. Strapped by financial stringency, the government had attempted to replenish the imperial treasury by issuing paper money, but the effort collapsed when excessive issue brought about steep inflation. Mortgaging the salt monopoly in return for merchant cooperation was an ingenious move to finance the garrisons.[29]

The weakness in this arrangement was that it took a merchant almost two years to transport salt from the grain-producing heartland of the lower Yangzi to the border, return to Nanjing, wade his way through bureaucratic delay and corruption to obtain his salt certificates, exchange them for his salt at the salt fields, and then transport it to the consumption districts, whereupon he would make arrangements for its sale. A division of labour rapidly followed, whereby rice merchants specialized in transporting grain to the border, and sold their salt certificates to specialized salt dealers in the lower Yangzi who now did not have to be involved in rice transport. This division between salt merchants and rice merchants put a price on the salt certificate. Although the legality of purchased salt certificates was always questionable, they came to be bought and sold, and, indeed, hoarded. Buyers of salt certificates, no doubt, were betting ultimately on the possibility of obtaining salt that might be sold at a profit, and, for this reason, the certificates may be regarded as a futures instrument, even though one should be careful not to exaggerate their transferability, as it is quite unclear how easily they were bought and sold.

A speculative element soon came to bear on the buying and selling of salt certificates. The salt certificate, naturally, was only as good as the amount of salt that might be put on the market by the Ming government, and as the government, like most governments, altered rather unpredictably the amount of debt that it was able to honour, the value of the certificates fluctuated. Openness was never a major feature of the Ming speculative market. At various times, when the government recognized that the surplus of salt certificates was deterring buyers, the certificates were regraded so as to allow priority of redemption for later issues. Quite often, powers at court — members of the imperial family, senior officials and eunuchs — were granted salt certificates that went beyond the normal quota, and such issues must have affected the value of salt certificates that had already found their way into private hands. In addition, the Ming government did not ever quite manage to quell salt smuggling, a problem that Ming officials well recognized as having been created by price differentials between government and illegally traded salt. Steadily declining prices for salt certificates played into the hands of the minority of merchants who successfully cornered the market. When, by the late Ming, in 1617, all efforts had failed and the emperor observed that he was deriving little benefit from the salt certificates, he abolished them altogether — in effect he repurchased them from holders at a fraction of their market value — and granted monopolistic rights to the households that were now emerging as major salt merchants.

No single stroke of the imperial brush could have created or destroyed a business tradition, but the decision of 1617 must have been one of those decisive moves that pushed China further along the path that would have made the emergence of banks and credit-bearing instruments more difficult. What the emperor did amounted to no less than abolishing the national debt, which he was indeed able to do in a single brush stroke. From now on, the right to trade in salt was granted as an act of imperial patronage and that alone. In return for patronage, merchants might be called upon to donate huge sums at imperial command. We do not know whether the amounts that were demanded in donation hence and the amounts that had had to be paid in graft before were substantially very different, but in terms of financial organization, salt certificates and imperial patronage entailed very different concepts. The salt certificate represented a debt that the government was obliged to honour, while a donation called for at imperial whim was arbitrary. Debts that were honoured by governments could become a foundation for the issuing of paper currency; the donation, at best, was another tax.

After it was reduced to patronage, the relationship between merchants and government in Ming and Qing China came to be known as "government-supervision and merchant management". This was how large-scale business enterprises came to be organized especially in the Qing dynasty, examples of which might include the Yunnan copper mines and the overseas trading operations conducted by the Cohong in Guangzhou. The concept was revived after the Taiping Rebellion (nineteenth century) in the series of activities that historians now refer to as the "self-strengthening movement". It was not until Sheng Xuanhuai, perhaps the most capable promoter of business enterprise in the late nineteenth century, introduced the idea of share capital into the operation of the China Merchants' Steam Navigation Company that once again, paper instruments came to be actively traded.

Commercial papers evolved: revolutionary bonds, along with rubber shares and lottery certificates of numerous varieties, thrived in the treaty ports in the last years of the nineteenth century and the early years of the twentieth century, and trade in shares and commodities thrived, primarily in Shanghai. I used to have in my holding a share certificate issued by a "nightsoil" collection company in Guangzhou in the 1930s, to cite only one instance to illustrate how far down the line stocks and shares might go in Chinese society once they were permitted. Just as important was the change in the popular literature: late Qing and Republican newspapers carried daily reports on business performance, exchange and interest rates, and a literature on these matters built up very quickly. Ma Yinchu, University of Columbia-trained economist who wrote and lectured on Chinese banking in the 1920s and 1930s, advocated the necessity for government legislation on credit-bearing instruments such as the bill of exchange, despite increasing state control of the banks and large-scale enterprises.[30] The outbreak of war in 1937, the war of liberation, and subsequent government policies changed all that, until revival came in the 1980s.

One can ponder, given a different set of circumstances, how business institutions might have advanced in late Ming China, *if*, as one might say, the emperor and his bureaucracy could not have put their stamp on the market of salt certificates as easily. Indeed, there was incipient capitalism in the sixteenth century. This was not the capitalism of the workshop but the capitalism of the sixteenth century futures market. Produced by accident, surviving by sufferance, it finally succumbed to the uncertainties of management by the imperial bureaucracy and then the whims of the emperor. The price that China had to pay was not that trade could not develop, for that went on for the greater part of three centuries to the best of anybody's imagination, but that when the time came for railways to be built and modernization programmes financed, the financial institutions were not in place to handle the gathering and transfer of funds on the scale required. The Chinese government turned to foreign banks, and that led to the highly political issue of imperialism.

3 Why Did the Chinese Economy Lag Behind?

The Chinese economy is said to have lagged behind in the nineteenth century for many reasons, not all of which are justified. Until the newspapers of Shanghai reported them in detail, inland famines were distant affairs for the coastal observer in China. Until then, Malthus might have speculated that population checks operated in China as they did in Britain, but they were not brought within the public view with any vividness or urgency.[1] If China appeared destitute in the second half of the nineteenth century, as compared to the perceived prosperity of the eighteenth, a large part of that appearance was illusory. Yet, whatever the state of sufficiency, whatever returns Chinese agriculture might yield on investment resources, industrialization made a very slow start in China. Armaments and some small-scale shipping were started in the 1860s and 1870s, but the railways and cotton spinning and weaving, almost universally the first rung onto steam power, were introduced, for the most part, in the late 1890s. Although exports boomed, China did not compete effectively in the international market place. Chinese sugar lost out to Javanese sugar, and even long-established silk-reeling lost out to late-comer Japan. By the 1910s, when Chinese people were, indeed, setting up factories in and near their major cities, China was saddled with a heavy foreign debt, the Chinese currency system had all but collapsed, and Chinese banks were at most in their infancy. Add to the scene the lack of any effective central government after the fall of the Qing dynasty in 1911, constant internal wars among the warlords, and by the 1930s, war with Japan, it is a wonder that there was scope for the 1920s to be referred to by historians as "the golden age of the Chinese bourgeoisie". It is an indication of the resilience of traditional business practices that, in the face of so much adversity, the economy could have been growing.[2]

The practices of traditional business were observed everywhere. They were demonstrated in the local markets, and amidst scenes of hawkers and stores selling rural produce. They were found also at the workshops, producing goods as varied as farm tools and electrical torches by the 1930s. The more modern-looking the enterprise, the more suspect traditional practices became. They existed side-by-side new technologies, but it was said the Chinese labour force had to adapt to its new demands. And most surely, the new technologies had to be imported. Ideas of steam power were totally alien to Chinese thought and practices. At the School of Naval Construction in the Fuzhou Shipyard in the 1867, Chinese students had to be trained in machine drawing, mathematics and physics, in French.[3] It took an entire generation at the Jiangnan Arsenal to produce the texts in Chinese.[4] New technology to China in the 1870s meant steam technology; China had itself invented most of the mechanical devices which went into spinning and weaving before steam.[5] Chemicals, steel, electricity and the internal combustion engine, products of the Second Industrial Revolution of the West in the later half of the nineteenth century, would catch on in China from the 1890s, but in the 1870s, it was on steam that Chinese technological modernization would stand or fall.

Steam Power and Technology

China acquired steam power with great difficulty. The reasons why it became so difficult for China to acquire steam power had to do with the state of traditional technology and nineteenth century politics. They are well-known to the China historian and should be quickly dealt with. For a start, China could not have invented the steam engine. Even though Joseph Needham argued that the Chinese blow furnace constituted the "pre-natal" history of the steam engine, China did not possess the technological edge needed to shape it into one. In this respect, the interest shown in the continuity of ideas by historians drawing from Needham has not been balanced by an examination of the technological base which could turn ideas into machines. Specifically, any comparison between Chinese and Western technology would have made it obvious that China did not invent the lathe, and, therefore, could not have achieved the precision which was introduced into the making of instruments by that particular tool in Europe. Not that the lathe would have made the steam engine, but it might be considered a precursor of the cannon borer which was adapted for the precision which James Watt needed for the piston in his engine. There should be no mistake between Watt's engine and the Chinese blow furnace. James Watt's shaft and piston were made of iron and the piston in the Chinese blow furnace was made of wood. The piston in the Watt and Boulton engine moved seven feet at each stroke, while the handle of the Chinese blow furnace no more than the length of the operator's arm. The motive force generated by the steam engine made it worthwhile to convert the linear motion generated by the piston into the circular motion which was then adopted in the railway engine, steamer and the factory. The Chinese blow furnace would have made it attractive to create a stronger motive force leading to more trap doors providing more air for a furnace, and hence to the replacement of the hand-operated piston by a series of cranks, in a more sophisticated version of the machine. Chinese workmen were precise when it came to woodworking or stone carving, but without the need to make clocks, guns and, especially, small arms, they had no need for a sophisticated machine tool industry directed towards metal working. China would not have invented the steam engine, because Chinese industry in the eighteenth century was moving along a totally different trajectory. Any suggestion otherwise demonstrates a total lack of appreciation for the difficulty of crossing technological hurdles presented by major shifts in technology.[6]

If China could not have invented the steam engine in the eighteenth century, might China have at least been able to learn to make one by the nineteenth? Again, the record of China in this effort is relatively clear. It is buried in the history of the "self-strengthening movement". This reformist period in Qing dynasty history stretched from the late 1860s to perhaps 1895, from the end of the Taiping Rebellion to China's defeat by Japan in the First Sino-Japanese War.[7] It began with the hope that China might emulate the West in a spirit of pragmatism, so that Western knowledge would be introduced "for use" while Chinese knowledge might be retained as "essence". It ended in a sense of failure and frustration upon China's military defeat. What we know as yet of the steam engine in this history can be told quickly. In brief, the steam engine could not have been introduced in China as a motive force except in relation to a machine, which in the mid-nineteenth century, would have been the railway engine, the steamer or part of the fitting out of a factory, such as a spinning mill, and all three innovations failed in China. In the 1870s, China resisted efforts to build a railway. In fact, the Qing dynasty government went as far as to purchase the demonstration railway which was built only to tear it down. No act of conservatism that, it was taken in defence of China's autonomy and in reaction to its fear that the railway might prove another Western incursion, all at a time when senior members of the Chinese officialdom were considering introducing the railway in north China. It was politics, therefore, which deflected the railway building effort.[8]

Likewise, politics came into factory building, but in a way which had more to do with late imperial understanding of how business related to the state than any prejudice against reform. No-one could have imagined for most of the Qing dynasty that factories might be built in China except by explicit permission from the imperial government. The imperial government granted a monopoly on operating the spinning mill to Zhili Province Governor-General Li Hongzhang, long recognized by the contemporary Western community in China as a modernizer. Yet, Li neither built the spinning mill nor let anyone else do so, and so machine-spinning did not develop in China until after the Sino-Japanese War of 1895. The war became a major landmark in China's economic development, usually because it is thought, by historians, that the peace treaty gave foreigners the right to go into manufacturing, but it might just as well be said that China's failure at the war led to the removal of Li Hongzhang from Zhili province, and from that time on, the opening of political patronage to all and sundry in the government.

Why China did not learn about the steam engine from the building of steamers is a more complicated question. The short answer, however, is that China did learn about steam engines from steamers, but too little and too late.[9] By the time the Chinese shipyards were in operation, in the 1870s, the West had moved on. The boiler makers who built the first steam engines in Britain were now engineers whose engines were built to the precision defined by an established mathematics. By the 1880s, breath-taking advances were also coming on stream in Western science and technology: the Second Industrial Revolution was supported by research in the laboratory and sustained on a mathematics in which algebra and calculus were an integral fundamental. In 1800, China might have acquired some of the industrial advances of the West with the minimum of change to the traditional curriculum, but to do so in the 1880s meant reforming school education to put a premium on a new mathematics and the forever elusive superiority of Western technology. Unlike Japan, which came to this stage of industrial development at the end of a political revolution, the Chinese literati considered education as the last bastion of its power, identity and continued existence. China was doomed, therefore, by the impossibility of timing. The great empire had to collapse before its economic structure might be put in place for the new technology to take root.

The Contractual Tradition: Its Strengths and Weaknesses

In the best nineteenth-century scenario, China would have acquired steam technology in stages. Like many third-world countries, it would have exported raw material and labour, opened up its mines, and, if its political structure could withstand the onslaught of social revolution which must follow, its leadership might have promoted education, law, the urban infrastructure, social stability and a more open society. Of course, that did not happen. Tradition stood side by side newly introduced institutions from the West, with few people comprehending the massive changes which were to engulf the entire society and having few ideas as to how they might come about. Looking back, historians have wavered between condemning Qing officials as conservatives and singing the praises of Confucianism as an ideology which might underpin East Asian economic development. Neither embodies a research strategy which answers the question why China had found it difficult to adopt steam technology. The answer has to encompass, not only what it might have been desirable for the country given any historian's particular bias, but also what traditional institutions were capable of doing and where they fell short in the nineteenth-century environment. The institutions of business and management, of course, would have been one area which merits particular attention, but traditional business methods have always been elusive and not given the attention they are due.

In search of traditional business institutions in imperial China, the historian must be prepared to recognize that, much as they were in Europe, they were created out of an environment in which business was not their expressed aim. The expressed institutional aims which were given pride of place in society at large were not economic but ritual.[10] Europe discarded the ritual cover for business in the long years between the Commercial Revolution (say the seventeenth century) and the Industrial Revolution (say the nineteenth century). China also went through a Commercial Revolution in the sixteenth century, but China did not, like Europe, arrive at an individualist ideology which made its way in business and in politics. Instead, China discovered the power of ritual as a tool for administration and extended it into business, of which more will be said. The point to be made here is that, compared with Western Europe, the substitution of business institutions for ritual came relatively late to China. To rest business on law rather than ritual was, in fact, one of the greatest impacts that the West made on China. This process took the whole of the twentieth century, and, to this day, has not been completed.

The objection will be raised by some among China historians that the twelfth century, rather than the sixteenth century, should be the turning point. Indeed, it can be, and if historians are allowed to generalize, we may find even earlier turning points. The further back one goes in time, however, the more the generalization becomes irrelevant for an understanding of China's economic lag in the nineteenth century, for, over time, the territorial concentration of Chinese state control shifted away from inland China to the economically active delta areas of south and central China. Until the twelfth century, most of what Chinese history books tell us about China took place to the north of the Yangtze River. After the twelfth century, population, and certainly wealth, concentrated to the south of the Yangtze. The politics of the state that concentrated to the north of the Yangtze was very different from that in which the centre of economic activities had shifted to the Yangtze but was governed from Beijing. An argument about Chinese business, therefore, faces the same general issue as faced by any argument about Chinese culture: it has to balance the rise of a corpus of ideas which posits the unity of the Chinese state with the means by which state administration spread over the expanding terrain that over four millennia became China. Substantial parts of China which became commercially active from the sixteenth century on did not come under the commercial advances of the Song dynasty.

It is inherent in this discussion that the advance of the state had been instrumental in promoting the business infrastructure. The extension of the Chinese state, indeed, provided the legal structure for the drafting of contracts, the ritual common ground from which corporate holding of property took off. Related to it was the spread of literacy which was required for writing contracts and keeping accounts, and litigating at the magistrate's office when disputes arose. One needs go no further for the hidden hand of the government process in historic Chinese society than taking note of the prevalence of land contracts. They are found in all parts of China where land was put to cultivation. They are so common, in fact, China historians take them for granted. We classify them, we probe the legal implications of their terms, we seek origins for the practice, we put it down to innate conservatism that land, rather than industry, should be regarded as a target of investment, and we do not ask why it was that most contracts had to do with land.[11]

The answer, of course, is amazingly simple. Written contracts extended with the implementation of Chinese local (that is to say, county-level) government, and they were used wherever Chinese government created titles for land. This is not to say that successive Chinese governments were concerned with promoting a land market. Quite the contrary, a persistent strain in Chinese administrative thought believed that land should be state property and that the less it was privately amassed, the better it was for the state. Yet, Chinese governments were interested in taxation, for which land was a ready resource, and techniques for land registration were developed for that purpose. So, wherever land was registered, property rights were created and it became possible for land to be sold. While China historians write about the ancient origins of land contracts, they, therefore, tell only half the story, and, that is, that for most of what now counts as China, land contracts were not known for most of Chinese history. Despite the early origins of written contracts in China, many of the highly commercialized parts of China did not use written contracts for land transfer until after 1500.

The fact that writing contracts was practically universal wherever Chinese local government was established says something about the nature of government. Written contracts were frequently employed in the Ming and the Qing for the transfer of property. The substantial number of written contracts known variously as *hetong* (agreement), *qi* (deed) or *heyue* (bond) that are available to China historians shows that they were used in the purchase of land, houses and people, in making loans and investment, in setting up business partnerships, in remitting money and in the execution of a wide range of ritual activities that included the numerous stages of the betrothal and wedding ceremonies as well as dealings with deities and spirits.[12] These documents were so commonly employed, in fact, that they were essential subjects included in popular handbooks that circulated both in print and in manuscript.

Yet, it is unclear if all contracts were equally enforceable in a court of law. The Chinese law code of the Ming and the Qing was designed primarily as a criminal code, and although some clauses might be extended into business matters, it would seem from the records available that the disputes that were brought into court dealt primarily with, in contemporary terms, "[matters relating to] marriage, household, and land", leaving out ostensibly partnership and money loans. The reason for this limitation probably had something to do with the expertise of the magistrate. The Ming and Qing magistrate, by virtue of his status as scholar, was required to be knowledgeable about family rituals, and because he served also as the chief county administrator, his taxation and land registration duties made him expert in land transaction. Business was not a subject that fell within his experience, and the magistrate would not normally be sensitive or sympathetic to the intricacies of business. The more common arbitrator for the merchant in Ming and Qing China would not have been the magistrate's court, but the merchants' guild, which drew up codes of practice for their members and which acted on behalf of the trade with outsiders and government. Existing documentation makes it far from clear how capable the guilds were in the settlement of disputes among members, but one would suspect that status and influence had much to do with conflict resolution.[13]

While written contracts were common, therefore, their efficacy in the organization of business has to be viewed in perspective. It has to be understood that they functioned without a well-defined commercial law, or even a customary law in which the concerns of business were very clearly spelt out except in moralistic terms. Let me cite as an example the limitation that was inherent in the Chinese partnership the following contract from a Ming dynasty Huizhou handbook:

> In view of the fact that wealth derives from partnership and results can be achieved by personal efforts, we (names) have agreed to pool our capital (*ben*) in search of profit (*li*). In the presence of a middleman-witness, we each put up so much capital; in a common mind and with lifted courage, we seek to enter business. All profits received shall be calculated face to face every year. Some funds shall be divided for use in our respective families, but capital shall be left so that the source [of our wealth] will not be exhausted. As for personal expenses, each [partner] is himself to prepare for them without expending funds that belong to the firm, so that the accounts will not be confused. For these purposes, we draw blood and make a pledge, and agree that it is fitting

all pain and happiness shall be shared and that [no profit] shall be
privately hidden for the fattening of one party. Any party that goes
against this agreement will be despised by both the deity and by man.
In order to provide a proof, two copies of this contract have been drawn
up, to be kept for future reference.[14]

One might suppose, at first reading of a contract of this sort, that
the reference to family expenses should only be incidental. I am
convinced it is not. Instead, I think it is a reflection that traditional
Chinese accounts lacked the mechanics to keep track of capital. I
think the provision, taken in conjunction with partnership
arrangements that we know of in other circumstances, for example,
in salt-mining in Sichuan or coal-mining near Beijing, illustrates well
the difficulties involved in the distribution of profit in partnership
in the absence of capital accounting. The detailed documentation
available on these operations shows that in these partnerships, general
principles in profit-sharing were adhered to that circumvented the
use of accounts and hence the need for agreement as to how they
must be kept for the calculation of monetary profits. For example,
the parties to the partnership might divide the products of the
enterprise (brine or coal) in proportion to their contribution, or
consign them for a flat fee under contract to a single purchaser,
mostly likely, one of the partners. In either case, the annual receipts
for the enterprise were relatively stable and the only accounts that
needed to be kept were running records of withdrawals made by
different partners. No other record of assets and liabilities was really
very necessary.[15]

It seems quite certain that Chinese businesses did not keep
capital accounts. Capital accounting does not appear in Takeda
Kasuo's careful comparison of sixteenth century Chinese and Western
accounting methods, while a survey into accounting practices in
Guangzhou in as late as the 1930s specifically noted that shop
accounts did not record the movement of goods in nearly as great
detail as cash transactions.[16] The absence of any means for capital
accounting was a general condition that must have been faced by all
partnerships. The annual profit as calculated from standard practices
would have balanced income and expenditure but would have made

no provision for bad debts or depreciation. In the absence of capital accounts, rules of the thumb dictated methods for fair division of profits without depleting business capital. Such rules of the thumb were not restricted to commercial activities. They were the same sorts of rules that applied in share-cropping, or in the management of the lineage estate, and, therefore, the reference in the partnership contract to drawing only as much of profit as was required for the family. It must have been known that the account balance did not represent the true profit.

The absence of a clear knowledge of the capital balance did not make shareholding on the long term easy, or, more pertinent to the development of the business firm, impersonal. Yet, shareholding of a sort did develop beyond the business partnership, and it came about via a religious connection. The religious trust that provided for sacrifice for ancestors and deities owned land, for it was the income from the land that ensured continuity of sacrifice. What is significant is that the trust would have been thought of as belonging to the ancestor or deity for whose sacrifice it had been set up, and the offerings given at sacrifice became, not a contribution made by descendants or worshippers but a gift to them, the descendants, from the ancestor or deity. The rules of worship, therefore, defined the corporation, and substituted for rules that might govern the management of equity. Yet, despite the right of all within the corporation to participate in sacrifice, the preparation for it, that included the management of the properties of the trust, had to be conducted by a small group of managers. From at least the early Ming, rotation among participating households had been the accepted practice. In the case of a trust held in the name of a deity, such household membership would have been defined at the time of its formation, and thereafter accrued to all descendants within the household. In the case of an ancestral trust, the rules of partible inheritance would have provided the rules of management, despite the prime position of honour accorded to the senior line of descent in recognition of which its members might be given an extra share of the sacrificial offerings but almost certainly not an extra year in the management of the trust. Accounts were drawn up at annual sacrifices, on which occasions management was transferred from one participating line to the next. The fact that land prices were assumed to be constant, that by law land held in the name of the ancestor might not be sold without agreement from all male descendants or their lines of descent, and that the rules of management were widely understood and accepted, made it possible for religious trusts to last very much longer than business partnerships.[17]

The ancestor or deity in the name of whom property was held, therefore, took on the character of a legal person. The ferries of Yuen Long district in the New Territories of Hong Kong, for instance, were in the nineteenth century held in the names of ancestors who had died some seven centuries earlier in the Song dynasty, and those in the know would have realized that the property was held by the corporate group rather than the individual.[18] There was clear understanding in law of what was entailed in this sort of ownership, for, in the case of the ferries, the lineage embodied the organization that provided the required management, for instance, in auctioning out the rights to manage annually. However, incorporating a trust in religious terms went beyond the realm of earthly law. The ancestors and the deities were subject to an order that belonged to a higher realm with which the emperor could intercede but not control. The religious trust, therefore, one might say, was one answer traditional China provided for the question of incorporation without the institution of the imperial charter. The emperor granted no rights that he could not withdraw, but the ancestors and deities might only be sustained by institutions that were founded to last for perpetuity. In this situation, one should not expect any long-standing capitalist institution to be held in the name of the individual. If there were long-standing capitalist institutions in Ming and Qing China, they would have been held in trust for ancestors and deities.

One might argue that the religious trust was predominantly a rural phenomenon, and that it was more practicable as a device for land management than in the conduct of commerce and industry. There would be much truth in this argument, but for three reasons, it should not be taken to mean that being primarily rural implied that it was primarily agricultural. Firstly, the religious aspect of the trust should not mislead us: an entrepreneurial objective is apparent in many trusts. In the Pearl River Delta, with which I am more familiar, the trusts were the agents through which capital was found and labour was recruited for land reclamation projects reaching back to the Ming dynasty. By the end of the Qing, shares held in some land-reclamation trusts were transferable. Secondly, it is well-known that merchants invested a considerable amount of their capital in land. Chinese historians have always assumed that land-holding was attractive because it was regarded as a safe investment, but that is no reason to think that the returns from investing in land-development projects were necessarily low. Thirdly, the Ming and Qing merchant made a clear distinction between the ongoing day-to-day trading functions of his business operations and his holding establishment. He traded in the name of his business (the "*hao*"), but held his property under a different name in a trust (the "*tang*"). The ritual basis on which the corporation was founded is illustrated in the Chinese character "*tang*". The *tang* is a hall. The Chinese character denoting it is the same character that would be used for an ancestral hall, or a hall in a temple complex. It stands for a physical building, even though in its business application, no building is necessarily implied. The *tang* holds property on the understanding that it is held for the maintenance of sacrifice to ancestor or deity, and as such, the property is often thought of as belonging to the spirit to whom sacrifice is offered. In both the sacrificial hall and the trust is rested an understanding of property rights.

The understanding that the sacrificial hall might stand for property holding can be readily understood with reference to Ming dynasty law. The law as originally instituted assumed that real, rather than fictitious, persons should be registered. However, as the law was applied, it became standard practice not only to retain the registered name on the record even long after the person so registered is deceased, but also for fictitious personal names to be registered. Names on the household registers, therefore, were readily regarded as names of ancestors, and the property acrrued to them, ancestral estates. Yet, household registration, obviously, did not apply to deities, who could not be registered as holders of property. For this reason, the common conception of property holding at a temple dedicated to the deity might well be at variance with legal understanding. Land was held under the names of temples, and Ming legal fiction would assume that because temples could not share in the corvee service required of household registration, tax and service which accrued to its holding might be assigned to households. In reality, the reverse is often true. Among the many exploits of the famous monk Hanshan Deqing at the Buddhist monasteries in early seventeenth-century Guangdong was sorting out the tax liabilities of the Nanhua Monastery, one of the important centres of Zen Buddhism. Local families which had control of its registered holdings were not delivering rent, but the monastery was held liable for tax, and, the result, as one might expect, was impoverisation of the sangha.[19] As Liu Zhiwei has very convincingly argued, by the sixteenth century, household registers dealt with tax accounts and not real households. Ming and Qing law was never revised to reflect this change.[20]

Chinese corporations, therefore, took a totally different approach to the maintenance of continuity from the Western firm. The partnership was not and not meant to be long-lasting, but the maintenance of ritual relationships in the religious trust had to be.[21] For this reason, the trust was a common device for use in holding property, by merchants and others alike, and inheritance practices would have ensured that at least some trusts would have survived as ancestral trusts. Businesses and trusts, or shares in them, could be passed on to descendants, and where they were not divided, would have been held in the name of the ancestor. The longer continuity that would be found in land-holding trusts possibly accounts for the greater amount of documentation that has survived to this day. The partnerships and the names set up for other businesses would have been much more transient.

Corporations which were formed with the ostensible purpose of offering sacrifice to the ancestor or deity did not rely on the keeping of accounts to maintain a fair distribution of profits, even though accounts were maintained and made public knowledge. They depended on the rules of inheritance. In the southern lineages — in the provinces of Guangdong and Fujian — each lineage segment, that is to say, descendants of the deceased ancestor in whose names the property was held, rotated their right to manage the estate, but sacrificial meats purchased with proceeds from the estate were distributed to all male members of the lineage.[22] The combination of the two practices results from the two interpretations of partible inheritance that was the common practice in these areas. Estates to provide for sacrifice were also established on contribution, and where the target of sacrifice was a deity rather than an ancestor, the management body took the form of a voluntary association (*hui*). Unlike membership to the lineage, membership to the voluntary association might be bought and sold, and the right of participation in the association, therefore, was frequently represented as a share (*fen*). Unlike family operations, holding operations conducted in the name of the ancestor tended to be long-lasting: lineages survived for centuries, their members being located in the same villages, holding land in the same areas, managing property under the same names that had been set up at the time of their origin. If they thrived, and many did, complications were introduced by what Maurice Freedman called lineage segmentation, which was less a segmentation process than the proliferation of land-holding trusts. The development often came with increase in wealth, which led to social inequality and not necessarily managerial inefficiency. The equivalent in temple holdings is less clear. Where land donated to the temple was managed by voluntary associations, the temples easily out-survived the associations. However, one suspects that the control of a temple could involve a highly charged political situation. Where rights and responsibilities were clearly demarcated, and where the local power structure was maintained, such as I have seen in the records of water-management associations in Shanxi and Fujian, disputes were settled within the framework of temple management.[23] Where they were not clearly demarcated, or where the local power structure was fluid, as was often the case, local warfare might determine how power changed hands.

Membership to the lineage or the temple alliance was restrictive, and so investment into and access to its funds would also be restrictive. Choi Chi-cheung's very detailed records of several

Chaozhou merchant families operating in the late nineteenth and early twentieth century in Shantou, Hong Kong and Southeast Asia illustrate how lineage funds tended towards internal, rather than, open banking.[24] Those very successful Chinese families invested in their sons and relatives' businesses, the new business firms maintaining close trading relationships with the investing parties and among themselves. The cross-holding of equity and credit adds to the trust that is built on family and kin relationships. The Chinese term for the resulting relationship, *lianhao* (linked firms), indicates that the operators understood the networking that was set up in the process. The maintenance of internal banking in this manner puts financial rather than administrative control at the centre of Chinese business management.[25] It allows for the operation over long distances that is found in some, especially overseas, Chinese businesses, and the spread of independent units of command would appear to be diametrically opposed to the vertical integration that became the norm after the rise of modern industry. Yet, to stress their common origin and lineage ties misses the boundaries set up for the network: outsiders cannot easily enter the internal bank that is effectively placed at the heart of the joint operations. These operations have proved very successful in trading, but when banks were run on these principles, as Ming and Qing banks were, the amounts of capital they could raise would be restricted.

Conclusion

The use of contracts and the establishment of corporate properties allowed for some definition of property rights, but they did not, by themselves, make for a financial market which could allow banking on a scale needed to promote the railway, mines, steamers or even factories in the world of steam. Native banking, which grew out of the use of contracts and incorporation through the lineage, operated on too small a scale to make much impact on the industrial financing that was needed. It could not have operated on a larger scale unless the Chinese government had instituted a national debt and thereby recognized that bankers had the right to issue paper money. The abolition of salt tickets towards the end of the Ming dynasty, therefore, was a decisive turn in Chinese business history. China gave up the finance market and turned instead to official patronage, continued into the next dynasty as "official supervision and merchant management". The right to engage in trade on a large scale was to be granted by imperial favour, in return for which, merchants were subjected to unspecified and arbitrary exactions in the form of gift. Taxation by fiat was, by definition, unpredictable. No bank of scale could have operated in that environment. That was China's main weakness in the nineteenth century. Businesses on a small scale could and did spring up on the China coast, in Southeast Asia, even North America, run by Chinese people, drawing on traditional practices, raising capital among themselves, relying on their social statuses and extra-commercial relationships to regulate elements of trust. Yet, the same practices could not have raised capital in shares and bonds from people who were strangers to one another, or attract deposits from wealthy people whose objective it was to keep their wealth from the knowledge of the officials. The impression that Chinese businessmen were adept at "networking" is, therefore, not unjustified. That was symptomatic of the lack of legal recognition or protection that they had the right to conduct business in areas where the state had not explicitly relinquished its privilege, and that must include the state's right to abrogate its debt.

The reasons for China's economic success in the eighteenth century were almost exactly the ones which made it lag in the nineteenth. Unless and until investment was needed in substantial amounts, ritual incorporation and private contracts served ably to mobilize resources. Yet, when the West brought the steam engine and the internal combustion engine, the telegraph, the railway, the spinning mill, the steam-driven flourmill and much more, private networks were inadequate as avenues for industrial finance. I am reminded of the review by the historian of technology, Ian Inkster, on the several books comparing east and west in economic development, including Frank and Pomeranz. The question, he says, does not lie in who was richer or more technologically advanced, but who at the point of contact could mobilize more wealth and more advanced technology.[26] This is where finance and banking come into the picture, and it is not only in the control of the sea, but in the different approaches to finance and banking that China and the West, and soon Japan, differed.

4 Company Law and the Emergence of the Modern Firm

The modern firm came about in China via one of three routes: it was sometimes the result of the privatization of central government enterprises; it was sometimes built upon the family firm; and in a few cases, it came about as an exertion of coordinated regional development.[1] It is possible to collapse these three routes to modernity into two, for regional development was in practice the privatisation of regional government enterprises combined with the evolution of regional family businesses into full corporations. Nevertheless, local government was essentially founded on principles very different from the centre, and the difference has to be noted.

It is easier to name some of the modern firms than either to put a very clear definition on the character of their modernity or to describe their prevalence. Among the various government enterprises that privatized would obviously have to be included China Merchants' Steam Navigation Co., the Hanyeping Co., and the Hengfeng Spinning Mill. Among the firms that grew from family businesses, it is possible to think of the Yong-an Company, Nanyang Brothers Tobacco, the Dalong Machine Works, and the numerous factories that were owned and managed by the Rong family. An example of a regional enterprise would be the Dasheng Spinning Mill and its associated businesses in Tongzhou (Nantong county, Jiangsu province) under the control of Zhang Jian. These are a minuscule fraction, of course, of China's modern firms from the late Qing to the Republic. They represent really the few cases on which, thanks to the effort of historians in China, source materials for historical research have been made available from the company archives, and the little that historians now know, far from making them complacent, underscores the great need for more research on business development in China.[2]

A common characteristic of these firms is that they belonged to a group that from the early years of the twentieth century referred to themselves as "companies" (*gongsi*). The term was popularized from nineteenth-century Guangzhou. In the eighteenth century, it was used by Chinese seafaring merchants with reference to the pooling of capital and from there it found its way into Chinese merchant organizations in Southeast Asia. In the 1830s and 1840s it was a translation for the British East India Company. It then became well-known in connection with communal institutions known to Westerners in Southeast Asia as well as China as secret societies, and was introduced into the national language by the popular media from the 1860s.[3] It represents more than the idea of a group of traders: the traditional term "*hang*" would have served that purpose very well, for "*hang*" denoted the combination of merchants trading in the names (*hao*) of their businesses, family firms and partnerships. But it was the word *gongsi* that by the 1870s, incorporated rather precisely the idea of a body of people coming together for the purpose of trade according to a charter that had been approved by government, an idea that would have been true to the meaning of the word as it applied to the East India Company. However, once generalized, its meaning changed to include all companies in which shares were held by a large number of shareholders. When company incorporation was introduced into China by the Company Law of 1904, the law was known as the *gongsi fa*.

The Company Law of 1904 redefined the role of the state in relation to business. Previous to this piece of legislation, state policy towards business was ambiguous. Imperial regulations ignored businesses on the small scale, but retained for the state the right to claim essential businesses as its monopolies. In practice, monopolistic rights, including the right to tax, were granted as privileges through patron-client connections that stretched from the imperial court down to the poorest rural market. In this setting, the state retained for itself the right to intervene in the market, which right was exercised by its officials with or without imperial approval. The uncertainty not only of state policies but also of their interpretation and execution by officialdom added to the risks that businesses had to face, and merchants reacted to such risks by seeking protection. If one argues from these policies that Chinese society was somehow opposed to trade, one argues in the face of the very active commercial development that took place in China from the late Ming to the Qing, the faith in silver expressed by all and sundry, and the strong awareness that trade brought profit and profit brought land that was written into the biographies of so many merchants that we know of. The net result of these policies was not the denigration of trade, but the denigration of the merchant, for the merchant traded at the sufferance of the official, who became the social model for the merchant to emulate. The numerous reforms of the last years of the Qing dynasty, of which the introduction of the Company Law was one, were designed to overhaul this balance of power. The abolition of the imperial examination, the recognition of commercial and agricultural associations, and the Company Law, tipped the balance in favour of the merchant. As in Europe, the Company Law replaced the idea of privileges granted by imperial charter with state recognition for private mercantile initiative in return for tax. From then on, private trade was the citizen's right, and if the state demanded more than a supervisory role, it was up to the state to nationalize.[4]

Historical developments in the West prior to the introduction of company legislation are instructive as a comparison for the experience of China, for the Chinese situation was not necessarily different from the European experience of the seventeenth and much of the eighteenth century. In Europe, trade, especially long-distance trade on a large scale, was conducted as state monopolies. Outside the areas defined as state monopolies, merchants traded on their own means or under private partnership arrangements. The state took an interest in the registration of private companies only when its stake in the chartered companies had receded, and when, because joint-stock ownership had proliferated, the idea of limited liability was gaining ground. In Britain, where not only did legal recognition for limited liability lag behind some other parts of

Europe, but also the Bubble Act made it a criminal offence to "presume to act as a corporate body", the possibility that the holding of a share in a partnership might imply unlimited liability did not impede the promotion of joint-stock companies in times of economic boom in the eighteenth and early nineteenth centuries. There, the joint-stock company might be incorporated by registration only from 1844 and limited liability was granted as a right only from 1855. It was, therefore, not the law that brought the business corporation into existence, but the widespread practice of shareholding that made the formation of the joint-stock company a reality. The law did not lead a social trend, but recognized it when it had to.[5]

With the very important exception that unlike the British monarch, the Chinese emperor refused to acknowledge the viability of a national debt, the business environment in China in the eighteenth century was probably not very different from Britain's. Partnership was rife, financiers sought investment opportunities, traders networked, land and commerce but not industry were acceptable to bankers as investment targets, and paper notes denoting ownership of one sort or another were traded. However, missing in China by the mid-nineteenth century was the experience that Western governments and legal systems had accumulated in relation to the operation of joint-stock companies. One might argue that had it not been for industrialization, the difference would not have been immediately translated into economic strength. It was not until the late nineteenth century that the investments needed for some industries, especially transport, were becoming excessive for individual financing, even though in the West, the industrial barons that dominated the new corporations were soon sufficiently wealthy to finance a good many of these on their own strengths. The need for private capital also went hand in hand with the need of the state to raise ever-larger tax incomes. The capital market developed in answer to these needs. Commercial instruments were created that might reduce the risks of investment, responsibilities were defined in the fully incorporated companies, while the state increasingly took on the role of guardian of shareholders' and depositors' interests in return for the right to tax. It should not be surprising, therefore, that when the business company — *gongsi* — appeared in China, it was received in a similar context.

The history of the incorporated company (*gongsi*) in China begins in the period known to historians as the "self-strengthening movement" of the second half of the nineteenth century. In the hopeful 1860s and 1870s, opportunities to introduce the incorporated company into China came about in two separate contexts. Proposals were made at various times to officials to permit incorporation, but these bore no fruit; yet Western merchants raised capital in China in the form of shares that were issued by companies incorporated under Western law, and were extremely successful.

The first articles of incorporation that were proposed to the Chinese officialdom were the ones drawn up in 1867 or 1868 by Yung Wing (Rong Hong), the Cantonese who was educated in the United States. The term *gongsi* appeared in this proposal for a shipping operation, and the capital for it was to be raised from 4,000 shares of 100 taels each. The face value of the share was therefore in what we may consider as a fairly low denomination, and even if shareholding could have been concentrated in few hands, one might argue that share-ownership by a wider public was built into the structure of the company. The company was to be managed by a board of directors elected from and by the shareholders, each share being entitled to one vote. There was to be an annual shareholders' general meeting during which the managing director would report on the previous year's finances and produce the books for examination. Dividend was to be paid on the shares out of profit within five days of the general meeting.[6]

The proposal was commented upon by the Zongli *yamen*, China's de facto foreign ministry at the time, that had accepted in principle ownership of steamships by Chinese nationals. However, in the aftermath of the Taiping Rebellion, if it was to be acted upon, it would have needed the support of the governors and governor-generals. Both the Zongli *yamen* and Governor-General Zeng Guofan, to whom the proposal was directed, were suspicious of foreign implications. Governor-General Zeng, of Jiangsu, Jiangxi and Anhui, easily the most powerful man in China in the 1860s who might push for reform, was concerned with building an arsenal, with the restoration of the economy of the loyal Yangzi after the rebellions and with the transport of tribute rice up to Beijing. He was a pioneer in the use of steamships in China in that he adopted them for warfare. He was also in support of working with merchants, not in steam navigation, but in the setting up of "offices for the recruitment of merchants" (*zhaoshang chu*) in the aftermath of the Taiping Rebellion in the salt trade.[7] In view of the support that was found for the "official-supervision merchant-management" mode of operation for a steamship company, which was then brought into operation after his death by his protégé and successor, Governor-General of Zhili Province, Li Hongzhang, the combination of events seems more than fortuitous. That later proposals should take the shape of an "office for the recruitment of merchants" for the transport of imperial tribute rice under the principle of "official-supervision and merchant-management" suggests intimate knowledge of official thinking on the part of the promoters of the enterprise. The China Merchants' Steam Navigation Co., as the enterprise was to be called, was founded on an understanding that government was comfortable with and that merchants believed they could tolerate. The official who was granted imperial sanction for the organization of the company, in this case, Governor-General Li Hongzhang, was to appoint the director, who managed the company together with leading merchants who were expected to be among the major shareholders.[8]

China Merchants' Steam Navigation Company was founded in 1873 on an authorized capital of 1,000,000 taels, which was increased in 1882 to 2,000,000 taels. Indeed, it competed with foreign shipping companies, but it drew considerable advantage from being the only Chinese-owned shipping company that was permitted by the imperial government and from the patronage of Governor-General Li. Besides the assured business of transporting tribute rice, it had access to government loans, it enjoyed relative ease in the acquisition of real estate needed for wharfing, that was to appreciate considerably in value in the decades to come, and goods carried on its ships were granted exemption from transit dues. Early reluctance shown by Chinese merchants to invest in the company reflects probably more a sense of caution towards the unknown than an assessment of the company's business potentials. According to Albert Feuerwerker, from about 1880, the reluctance of the Chinese mercantile community to put its capital into the China Merchants' Steam Navigation Co. surprisingly gave way to a considerable demand for the company's shares, and although Feuerwerker argues that China Merchants' Steam Navigation shares were essentially held through the private networks of the directors, as K. C. Liu and others have shown, by the 1880s, the Shanghai market was rife with speculation on shares of precisely the sort of official-supervision merchant-management enterprises that China Merchants' Steam Navigation was. After China Merchants' Steam Navigation, major enterprises that raised substantial capital from Shanghai included the Kaiping Mines and the ill-fated Shanghai Spinning Mill.[9]

The speculative fever of the 1870s and the early years of the 1880s extended out of an international economic trend. One might think of it as an indication of economic imperialism, but this term, far from distracting attention from Chinese entrepreneurial activities, should put at the centre of historical discourse the outburst of effort in seeking opportunities to invest and the contradictions that appeared in China when the state had yet not declared its abstention from the opportunities that modern industry was promising. In the treaty ports of the 1870s, the interests of the Chinese merchant in the pursuit of profit were complementary to his Western counterpart's. It was generally known that Chinese merchants invested in Western enterprises: possibly 70 percent of all Western shipping was financed by Chinese merchants, and the figure of the compradore that became the linchpin in the Western merchant's dealings with the Chinese was crucial not only as buyer and marketing executive but also as financial broker and at times financial controller.[10] There can be little doubt that the bulk of this investment went through trust that had been established via private channels and no questions were asked if the business was incorporated anywhere. Such, it seems, was the status of the Shanghai Steam Navigation Co., the American steamship company that in 1877 was purchased by China Merchants' Steam Navigation at a price of 2,200,000 taels.[11] It was said in both Hong

Kong and Shanghai that through the 1860s and 70s, the Chinese merchant was doing very well and the financial boom of the 1870s was fuelled by his capital as much as that of his Western counterpart's.

One might argue that incorporation was immaterial to the Chinese climate. That view might be true of the 1860s, but would not take account of a number of changes to commercial practices in the 1870s. To begin with, company registration on the China coast was, by the 1870s, a reality. Following changes in British companies legislation, a Companies Ordinance had been adopted in Hong Kong in 1865, thereby making limited liability a possibility.[12] Secondly, some of the legal implications of registration became quite material, as company promoters were soon to learn. Many companies founded in the 1860s and 1870s dealt in shipping, insurance and banking, and for them the protection of limited liability must have been inherently attractive.[13] Despite the opposition of prominent members of the mercantile community as the bill was read in the Legislative Council, once it was passed, the ordinance was resorted to by none other than the Hongkong and Shanghai Bank when it was founded. Its board of directors, even in those days, was made up of some of the most influential Western merchants in Hong Kong.[14] Thirdly, the Western companies that raised share capital on the China coast were given considerable publicity in the newspapers. News reports of court trials, both in the consular courts and in the courts in Hong Kong, together with minutes of annual and special meetings of corporate bodies, were providing the raw material for a legal culture that was coming into shape at the treaty ports. Fourthly, shareholding was also becoming more extensive. Into the 1870s, it is true that much share capital was raised through private connections, but it was no longer necessary to leave matters entirely in the hands of the middleman. Jing Yuanshan, manager of the Shanghai Cotton Cloth Mill, advertised the prospectus of the mill in Shanghai newspapers and raised the needed capital.[15] The Chinese historian Zhang Guofei sums up the development from the 1870s to the 1880s succinctly when he says, "It was only after the 1880s that the gathering of capital began to break through the narrow confines of merchant groups, friends and relatives, and made the merchants of all the major cities in the country the targets to be won over."[16] Despite the collapse of the Shanghai stock market in 1883 and the caution that was raised about the joint-stock companies, by 1890 the first stock exchange to begin in China was opened in Shanghai.[17]

It is easy, though, to exaggerate the transition in investment patterns from the 1870s to the 1880s. Investment in company shares could still not have absorbed more than a tiny portion of the available capital in China. Moreover, the new government enterprises and joint-stock companies were not yet commanding so much confidence that the new entrepreneurs would have felt secure about leaving the bulk of their wealth in company shares. Opportunities were abundant in the traditional sector, and risks had to be spread. When he went bankrupt in 1883, the hitherto very successful compradore Xu Run owned eight pawnshops and more than two million taels worth of real estate in Shanghai, in addition to his 1,275,000 taels in shares.[18] Into the 1890s when Sheng Xuanhuai was director of China Merchants' Steam Navigation Company, he was accumulating, aside from China Merchants' Steam Navigation stock, also real estate, while he also speculated, through his wife, on the rice market.[19] Tradition-bound attitudes were not replaced by shareholding in the modern companies. Rather, it was shareholding that was being absorbed into the Chinese business tradition. Quite aside from questions of nepotism, it was built into the shareholding structure that major shareholders might be directly involved in managing branches of the company. China Merchants' Steam Navigation made it a rule that major shareholders were to be appointed branch managers and at the Kaiping Mine they might appoint their own overseers.[20] Public shareholding did not bring about a division of ownership and control in China as in the West, nor did it reduce the impact of the family on ownership.

There were, consequently, contradictory trends in the evolution of the share market. Government officials were aware of the market's potential in raising much needed capital, while the market gained strength because the institutions of business, as long as they were registered outside Chinese jurisdiction, were taking a form that might free them from arbitrary government decisions. In the late 1870s and the 1880s, these tendencies came to a head in the question of funding for manufacturing: by treaty, Westerners obtained the right to trade in China but not the right to manufacture. The silk filature that began in Guangdong province probably escaped official control partly because it was small, and partly because it was totally Chinese-owned. A spinning mill for the manufacturing of cotton yarn, assured of a market in China, would have required larger capitalization and would have been the test case for the Chinese officialdom's willingness to allow the market to take its own course. It seems that the initiative had come in 1878 from Chinese merchants, but from an early stage, Western merchants had been interested in promoting Western spinning machinery and Jardine Matheson had had a hand in planning the mill that sought approval from Governor-General Li Hongzhang. The capital was raised in Shanghai in 1882 to the excess of its authorized capitalization, while in response to Governor-General Li's request, the imperial court gave it a monopoly on machine-spinning that was to last for ten years. However, the successful capitalization was followed immediately by the collapse of the Shanghai stock market, during which it was learnt that Zheng Guanying, who had been responsible for raising much of this capital, had collected a third of the subscriptions not in money but in shares, and loaned out another third for his own personal benefit. Starved of an operational capital, new shares had to be raised in 1887, an exchange of shares having to be arranged on a reduced scale for previous issues. Other scandals were to follow, while the spinning mill came to naught as it burnt down in a fire in 1893.[21]

Thus, there was more than the issue of stemming official control in the emergence of joint-stock operations in China. Their published comments to the contrary, in the 1880s, merchants tended not to be opposed to drawing on the resources of the capital market to strengthen China's industrial and commercial enterprises, the more important of which were rapidly growing into military-industrial complexes. Governor-General Li Hongzhang's purview included arsenals, a shipping company, the Kaiping and other mines, China's telegraph and now a monopoly on cotton-spinning. With news that the railway was to be built in China, a second military-industrial empire was taking shape under the tutelage of Governor-General Zhang Zhidong. Consisting of the Daye Iron Mine, the Pingxiang Coal Mine and the Hanyang Ironworks, this empire would manufacture China's railway tracks and would have done so but for the fact that the wrong machinery had been ordered.[22] Governor-General Zhang added another innovation, the mint, which was to debase China's coinage.[23] Much of the record we have of official intervention in the operation of these government-sponsored companies reflects the demands of the merchant managers to be given a free hand in their management of these operations. However, lacking in their records is any discussion of a matching need for accounting and audit control. Given the record of some of these managers, business autonomy without accountability would set them not very far from sole private proprietorship.

Historians have noted often that the pace of China's industrialization quickened after the Sino-Japanese War and the reasons for that can be readily stated. It was partly the result of the Treaty of Shimonoseki with Japan, the terms of which, by the most-favoured nation treatment, were extended to other treaty powers. The clause that made an impact on China's industrial establishment granted the right to foreigners to build factories within China, and that removed any reason for officials to maintain a monopoly. Another part of the reason was political. The defeat also brought about the downfall of Li Hongzhang, and with that a reorganization of his sphere of influence, bringing to the fore Yuan Shikai in the military regime and Sheng Xuanhuai in the economic. Coincidentally, it also brought Zhang Zhidong for a short while into Nanjing as Governor-General of Jiangsu, Jiangxi and Anhui, and while there he took an immediate interest in development around Tongzhou (present-day Nantong county) that launched Zhang Jian onto his regional enterprise centred on the Dasheng Mill, and which made Tongzhou an industrial centre in Jiangsu into the Republic. The treaty also brought to a head China's railway development, a much discussed issue inside and outside official circles from the 1880s with the assured implication of the need for investment funds. Moreover, the terms of the Treaty of Shimonoseki led to the

"Scramble for Concession", the Boxer Uprising and then the Boxer Protocol, by which not only was an inordinate debt imposed on the Chinese government but it was also made to accept Western demands to reform the commercial law. The overall psychological effect of defeat was, no doubt, itself conducive to a sense of urgency with which the Qing government greeted reforms. Along with announcements for prospective constitutional changes, the imperial examinations were abolished, chambers of commerce were to be encouraged, the criminal code was to be modernized and the entire legal framework overhauled.

The impact on business organization of all these changes was that Li Hongzhang's financial hierarchy was to devolve into private enterprise, family firms that had successfully established themselves were to become modern enterprises, and regional developments began to take on a new life.

The burst of economic activities in China from 1895 to 1911 was spectacular. Among the many differences from the previous decades, the age when a few senior officials might serve as patrons for a large number of commercial operations was passing; there was no-one but Zhang Zhidong who might succeed Li Hongzhang, and Zhang had no successor at all. In their place to provide patronage was the next generation of senior officials, well connected and adept at bureaucratic operations perhaps, but who could readily be removed by imperial command. Some second-generation officials, for instance, Zhang Jian, Zhou Xuexi and Nie Qigui, became merchants and industrialists. It is true that large-scale privately owned industrial enterprises without overt claim to government sponsorship could now come into existence, but it must not be thought that the passing of a few dominating characters signified that patronage was giving way to the free market. The decline of imperial authority after 1895 and the absence of a senior officialdom that could stamp their character on substantial portions of the bureaucracy brought about genuine decentralization of power. The result was that the structure of patronage broadened, not that it faded away.

The involvement of the family firm in modern industry and business requires a study of its own which will have to take into account the readiness with which China accepted modern technology and the control of equity within the context of the Chinese family. Suffice it to note the most obvious, that is, that the import of technology required capital, and investment in technological import was risky, especially before 1895, when government policy had not made it clear that such investment was tolerated. To minimize such risk, Chinese merchants invested in foreign firms, all the while as Western as well as Chinese merchants cautiously tested the tolerance level of the officialdom. Characteristically, industry started under these conditions required only low start-up capital and promised rapid profit. The most successful of these would have to be the steam filatures of Guangdong, and the machine works that serviced the treaty port shipping industry.

The success of the steam filature in Guangdong can be told in the volume of steam filature silk that was exported before 1895. The steam filature was a relatively simple device that provided a constant supply of hot water for treating the silkworm cocoon as the human hand attached the silk thread onto spindles that were turned by the human foot. The silk that resulted was considered to be of a high quality and fetched a good price. The factories were set up in villages where silk spinning had traditionally been carried out by women. It was introduced into Guangdong in the 1870s, and faced considerable and sometimes violent opposition from hand-reelers in the 1880s. However, the industry persisted, and, as a result, even before 1895, when filatured silk became a permanent feature of export. By 1900, it was filatured and not hand-reeled silk that became the major portion of export from Guangdong. The lower Yangzi area took up the steam filature much more slowly and it was only in the 1910s that filatured silk export exceeded the hand-reeled variety in this area.[24]

The first privately owned and managed machine works must have been founded early, even though the clearly documented cases date only from the 1860s in Shanghai. One has to think of the port areas in the cities that were opened to foreign shipping as shanty towns, with their ship chandlers, repairmen, stevedores (known rather impolitely as "coolies" in China), and the processing industries. The machine works contracted from the docks, but branched out very rapidly into related industries. Fachang Machine Works advertised in the *Shenbao* in 1873 for its gold-plating service. By 1877, it offered for sale lathes it was able to make. In 1884 it built its first steamship.[25] Aside from shipbuilders and repairers such as Fachang, other workshops in the 1880s produced cotton gins and steam filatures. These firms started with little capital; of the twelve workshops started between 1866 and 1890 that historians in Shanghai have been able to document, none began with more than 500 *yuan* (1 *yuan* was equivalent to 0.72 tael). Seven of the initial owners had formerly been owners of traditional metal works, two came from shipping or the docks, two were traditional merchants, and one had come from a senior appointment in the China Merchants' Steam Navigation Co.[26] The same tendency continued after 1895. More machine works were set up, but their capitalization, as before, remained tiny, with the exception of Dalong that was founded on 10,000 *yuan*, and that was to become the most successful of them all. These factories no doubt enjoyed some degree of trade credit, but tended to be self-financing. Into the 1930s, Dalong depended primarily on its own resources, which, over the years, had grown not only because its industrial capacity had expanded, but also because the Shanghai real estate that it owned had considerably appreciated.

The relaxation of control after 1895 had its immediate impact on the scale of private investments. Before 1895, not a single private enterprise was founded that was capitalized at anywhere near 100,000 *yuan*. Between 1895 and 1904, the year the Company Law was introduced, aside from the mines, 83 enterprises had been started with a capital of more than this figure, of which there were 9 spinning mills, 28 steam filatures in the lower Yangzi area (the ones in Guangdong continued to be small), 8 flourmills, 1 match factory, 3 machine works, 4 oil presses, and a winery, founded by the overseas Chinese financier Zhang Yuquan.[27] The year 1895 also saw the first attempt to implement government financing for private industry: Zhang Zhidong, as Governor-General of Jiangsu, Jiangxi and Anhui, received imperial approval to divert the repayment of merchant loans (*xijie shangkuan*) to the financing of industrial enterprises in Jiangsu.[28] The move could hardly have been very popular. Merchants were not at all enthusiastic and subsequent memorials show that merchants preferred to raise their own capital. Nevertheless, the attitude of officialdom had changed. The emphasis after 1895, now increasingly noted under the term "commercial war" (*shangzhan*), was that China should recover rights to the exploitation of economic resources that had been lost to foreigners.[29] Officials were actively engaged in promoting industry and merchants were more than willing to oblige.

Again, it is easy to misrepresent a gradual transition after 1895 as a sudden breach with the past. The new policy had not spelled an end to the close personal involvement of officials in private enterprise. Zhang Zhidong in Hubei, and other governors and governor-generals in Shanxi, Zhili, Shaanxi, Xinjiang, Xichuan, Guangdong and other provinces continued to promote industries on the official-supervision merchant-management model. A notable example would have been the spinning and weaving complex in Hubei started by Zhang in 1894 on a capital of one million taels of official and 500,000 taels merchant funds, which was subsequently in 1902 rented out for merchant management on terms that included transit tax remission.[30] Another example would have been the Sulun Silk Filature in Jiangsu, originally designed to be a merchant enterprise that would be financed with a government loan, that, upon the lack of merchant interest in the loan, became an official-supervision merchant-management enterprise, and that was rented out to merchants after 1902. In Hangzhou, the terms of incorporation of a machine flourmill, towel-knitting and match factory advertised in 1900 claimed that it had obtained official approval for a ten-year monopoly in all of Zhejiang, even though it did not raise enough capital ever to go into operation.[31] In Hunan, the Baoshan Company, according to a memorial by Zhang Zhidong in 1897, was founded on share capital raised by Hunan gentrymen but which was taken over as an official enterprise by 1898, and was apparently sustained on control exerted over local saltpetre manufacture.[32] The centralization of formerly scattered saltpetre workshops under the Baoshan Company was initiated by the province-wide militia office (*tuanlian zhongchu*), and the involvement of this body indicates a strong sense of collusion between provincial gentrymen and provincial officialdom.[33]

Some degree of gentry-official collusion is probably what one should expect in the aftermath of Li Hongzhang's demise. The fragmentation of the patronage structure that had formerly come under Li had brought about as many independent patrons for industry as there were local officials, but as enterprises developed local roots they also tended to be locked into local influence networks. The intricate relationships that Zhang Jian was to develop with Tongzhou illustrate this recent trend.

The Dasheng Spinning Mill was founded by Zhang Jian after he was appointed by Zhang Zhidong, Governor-General of Jiangsu, Jiangxi and Anhui, to promote commerce in that area. It was originally intended that capital would be raised among merchants in Shanghai and in Tongzhou. When capital raised privately fell far short of what had been expected, Zhang Jian turned to provincial officials for financial support. He received little, except for an allotment of spinning machinery that Zhang Zhidong had initially ordered for Hubei that had been lying idle in Shanghai. In return for the machinery, the provincial government was to be given a 50 percent stake in the company. The injection of official assets did not make it easier to raise capital. On the contrary, it led ultimately to the withdrawal of the Shanghai directors of the company. By 1897, a new arrangement had to be reached with Governor-General Liu Kunyi, specifying that the contribution of the government did not empower it to appoint the directors.[34] The day seems to be over when a senior official could provide overall patronage and make his appointments in enterprises that were founded under his aegis.

None of the industrial enterprises so far described, however, matched the capitalization that was to be needed for China's railways. One of the shortest railways to be built, begun in 1906 and completed in 1909, the 36-mile Xinning line in Guangdong, cost its promoters 2.5 million *yuan*. In this instance, the promoters were overseas Chinese and much of the funding was raised in America. However, the news of the day was dominated not by projects of this scale, but by the attraction of long-haul railway construction and the redemption of lines that had been constructed under foreign loans and that had consequently been committed to foreign management. The redemption of the Canton-Hankow line in 1905 alone cost ten million taels.[35] Much of the new capitalization was still raised through foreign loans, and Quan Hansheng is undoubtedly correct to argue that it was because of the weakness of the internal capital market that central and local governments only raised the much needed capital by imposing tax surcharges.[36] However, Wellington Chan has probably captured the mood of the years immediately after 1900 with the following: "For a while during the 1900s, it appeared that the promoters of private railways had stumbled upon a strategy which, in one stroke, would eliminate both hurdles — excessive control and inadequate funding. By appealing to an aroused populace's sense of national pride and outrage against Western encroachment, these promoters successfully organized widespread public subscription campaigns, raising millions of taels as investment capital. The same campaigns also generated such a popular movement of potentially revolutionary force that the state was driven out of the railways."[37] When the state tried to reassert centralized control via the Ministry of Communication and Transport in 1910, as Quan Hansheng points out, the Revolution of 1911 broke out.

The tendency towards a legalized basis for commerce and investment arose, therefore, in the early 1900s with the need to gather capital. Hence the stock market, hence the need to regulate shares. None of this evolved in a vacuum: in a very real sense, provisions for company incorporation and open purchase of stock and shares implied not the reassertion of formal state authority but the devolution of the power of patronage exerted by individual members of the officialdom. However, it is necessary to see also that long before a legal basis was created by legislation, the practice of bringing disputes to law was being publicized. Moreover, because Westerners in China tended to see the law as one of the issues by which China might be opened for more trade, it was not only publicity but diplomatic pressure, very effective when it coincided with treaty revision at the end of a war in which China had lost, that was brought to bear on the Chinese government in favour of commercial legislation. The net result was a successful transformation of modern China's culture, albeit only for several decades.

Some of the pressure for legal reform had come from Westerners on the China coast, for even before the Boxer Uprising, treaty revision was in the air. George Jamieson, who in the 1890s went into the question of Chinese mercantile law recalled with a sense of frustration in 1919: "The code [*Da-Qing lu*] gave no assistance under this head, and the various collections of decided cases which I consulted, did not help much. Details of crime and punishment were abundant in every possible variety, but of commercial law not a word was said."[38] Matters came to a head in 1897 and 1898, when the refusal of the Shanghai *daotai* to enforce the liability of Chinese shareholders alarmed Westerners. The issue had arisen over two cases brought before the *daotai* concerning the liability of Chinese shareholders to pay calls on their shares in the Western-registered Bank of China and Japan upon the bank's liquidation. In both cases, while Westerners considered that the shareholders were liable, the *daotai* considered that the treaties had not provided for the holding of shares by Chinese nationals in Western companies. It was concluded, therefore, depending on different English-language reports of the judgements, either the holding of shares by Chinese people in Western companies was illegal, or their liability was unenforceable in a Chinese court. The China Association in Shanghai, quite alarmed at the judgement, wrote to the British ambassador in 1898 in the following terms: "The judgement of the Taotai [*daotai*] goes far beyond the immediate question of share contracts, of which it was the outcome. It is plain that it strikes at the very root of all commercial relations between Chinese and foreigners, in that the validity of all contracts now becomes dependent upon the ruling of Chinese courts, based upon a shadowy, and to us unknown law."[39] In 1899, it wrote to the Foreign Office, in language reminiscent of petitions sent by British merchants to Parliament before the First Opium War, "Everything points to approaching industrial development in China, on an important scale. Foreign and Chinese capital is certain to be more and more associated. Numerous questions of great commercial importance are almost certain to arise, between foreigners and Chinese, which will demand settlement by a competent court; yet there exists in China neither law to regulate, nor tribunal which can be relied upon to adjudicate fairly in cases of difficulty of dispute. Charges of incapacity are, in fact, frequently launched from the throne; though, commonly, under the guise of denunciations, of clerks and underlings for rapacity and extortion."[40] These comments culminated in the Mackay Treaty of 1902. Article 4 of the treaty dealt with the holding of shares in Western-registered companies by Chinese persons, and Article 12 even held out the hope of the ending of extraterritoriality on the condition that China would reform its legal practices.[41]

In view of the concern for Chinese legal reforms, it should be somewhat surprising that the Chinese Company Law of 1904, so obviously a response to the Mackay Treaty, received little interest in the English *North China Herald*, even though it was reported in full in the Chinese *Shenbao*. The sort of legislation that Westerners were particularly concerned with in China was not the registration of Chinese companies, but mining and patent regulations, both of which were given priority by the newly formed Bureau of Agriculture, Industry and Commerce, and covered in some detail by the *Herald*. The impetus that led to the Company Law was probably Chinese: Wu Tingfang himself, the first Chinese person to become an English barrister and a vice-president of the bureau who with little doubt had direct charge of the drafting of the law, probably played a strong hand in the matter.[42] Wu was close to legal circles in Hong Kong, where his brother-in-law, Sir Kai Ho-Kai, barrister, was a member of the Legislative Council. In Hong Kong Chinese circles, China's need for constitutional and legal reform had been felt through the 1890s.

Yet, the practicalities of business had been enforcing a discipline of their own. Customary practices notwithstanding, Chinese as well as Western merchants did resort to the court to settle disputes arising out of contracts. There was possibly an undercurrent in Shanghai and other treaty ports for partnerships to increasingly take the form of joint-stock operations through the 1890s and into the early 1900s. *Shenbao* on 2 February 1904 reported a case heard before the Shanghai *daotai* in which what was essentially a partnership described itself as a *gongsi*, sold shares, went into liquidation, and then raised new shares to continue business. The suit, as can be understood, was brought by a shareholder who had bought shares before the liquidation of the company via a middleman. The magistrate did not hold the middleman in this instance liable, but that was only one judgement in a long-standing legal issue over the interpretation of the liability of the broker as principal or agent in a transaction. Jamieson quotes a Shanghai case in 1885 that was finally settled by the Privy Council in Britain in favour of Sassoon & Co.[43] It is significant that Chinese merchants were to learn that they could resort to the same channel to their advantage. In 1907, when the newly established Shanghai General Chamber of Commerce commented on the need for a commercial law, it referred to a case brought by Chinese merchants to the Privy Council in which the decision went against the Chartered Bank of India, Australia and China for liability arising from a compradore who absconded.[44]

The Company Law of 1904 by which the Chinese government gave recognition to company incorporation and limited liability was, therefore, the last of a long series of events that brought the modern company into existence in China. The significance of this chain of events rests not on any reform of business management as such, but on the greater ease by which capital might be raised and corporate responsibilities might be defined. As the law was enacted, also created were a number of institutions, notably the Ministry of Commerce in the government (which soon developed into the Ministry of Agriculture, Industry and Commerce) and the chambers of commerce among merchants that were to put official-merchant relationship on a new footing. There was no rush to register companies.[45] Most businessmen, no doubt, went on as they had done before, relying on their own and their family funds, as well as contributions from small groups of partners. However, for one reason or another, some companies did register. It would take time for fund-raising on the open market to sink in. That was not to come until well into the Republic.

5 The Responsibility System and Enterprise Reform

Economic growth from the 1870s continued until the early 1930s. By then, the World Depression caught up with China; production slumped and the monetary system came under attack. Had this book been concerned with the economic record rather than the narrower theme of the institutional structure which underpinned the economy, it would be necessary to examine the role of Chinese banks in the monetary reforms to follow and the tightening of government control in the last years of the 1930s. The shock of economic collapse, however, was rapidly superseded by the outbreak of war with Japan (1937 to 1945), and then the civil war between the Chinese Communist Party and the Guomindang Party. When the civil war ended with the success of the Chinese Communist Party and the establishment of the People's Republic in 1949, hyperinflation ruled.

The new government of China in 1949 brought inflation under control very quickly. Through the imposition of rationing, the abrogation of foreign debts and very soon afterwards, the collective ownership of land and the nationalization of business and industry, it brought the economy out of civil war depression. By the end of the 1950s, however, disaster struck. The Great Leap Forward of 1958 led to famine, and the few years of relaxation immediately after were followed by the Cultural Revolution, which began in 1966. The first three years of extremism against any sign of capitalism, which included the practice of accounting in state-owned enterprises, ground the economy to a halt. Most of the 1970s was marked by economic shortage and austerity. Against this background, at the Eleventh plenum of the Ninth Party Congress, Deng Xiaoping, newly restored to a position of power, instituted a totally new direction for the economy in advocating special economic zones — in which foreign investment was encouraged, and the "responsibility system" in agriculture, in effect, permitting the use of private contracts. Events since have proved the plenum to be a major political and economic turning point in the history of the People's Republic of China. Without under-rating its importance, this chapter will show how, yet, it followed on from the history of institutional changes from the sixteenth century.

The Chinese Communist Party and Economic Reform

To appreciate China's economic development since 1949, we have to begin with the Chinese Communist Party in war time. The Chinese Communist Party at war was a remarkable phenomenon. Perhaps discipline and ideology sum up best the driving forces behind its success. However, the same can be phrased in terms of the structure of the party, in particular the highly concentrated command that was exerted through the party secretaries in party cells. Chairman Mao Zedong described the party's function in terms of democratic centralism; it embraced the ability to guide as well as to absorb the desire of the masses, to define policy objectives, to generate discussion, and to mobilize support for their implementation. In this respect, one might think of the Chinese Communist Party as an independent command hierarchy, running parallel to the command hierarchy of the Chinese state. Command hierarchies work best in times of crises: preparation for war was high on the Chinese government's agenda for most years since 1949 until the early 1970s, even though one of the greatest achievements of the post-1949 government has been to give China the longest period of internal peace since the collapse of the Qing dynasty.

In China, the political party emerged only from the early twentieth century. How it evolved in conjunction with the Chinese state is a subject of considerable interest to historians and embedded in it are some fundamental tenets that ruled the evolution of Chinese business. The milestones in this history are the revolutionary situations in 1911, 1927 and then 1949. By this I mean that the governments set up in those respective years saw themselves as inheritors of revolutionary traditions, and accorded to their success the success of ideologies on which they sought their legitimacy. As every modern Chinese history book puts it, 1911 heralded republicanism, 1927 nationalism and 1949 communism. As every history book also implies, although some express this facet of government evolution more clearly than others, every one of the three stages proved to be a transition towards greater centralization of government authority, which authority was exerted on business as on many other aspects of social life.

Inherent in the increasing concentration of authority in revolutionary governments is possibly one of the greatest contradictions of twentieth-century history, not only in China but also in many other parts of the developing world. Twentieth-century governments that emerge in the name of social revolutions seek to build their authority on the predictability that might be offered by the party bureaucracy. But the party bureaucracy is only predictable because as command flows downwards, it prevents opposition views from filtering upwards. The more centralized the command structure, therefore, the more stress there has to be on the ability of the centre to command, and this ability has to be justified not by the party machinery's capability to reflect the popular view, but by a mystical popular acceptance of the party's privileged position to know, which is demonstrated by the party's access to power through revolution. In the sense that the party centre's ability to command has to be unquestioned, ideology has to become a religion. For Marxism, with its claim on a scientific basis to the laws of history, this is very ironic indeed.

The crisis of the revolutionary ideology in the twentieth century, therefore, is not the crisis of centre versus periphery, socialist planning versus capitalist market, and not even one-person-one-vote democracy versus dictatorship, but a crisis of a claim for knowledge and of its failure. Because the centre, on the basis of its ideology, failed to deliver the promised consequence of the revolution, the ideology itself came into question. In the shift from the principle of certainty in the revolutionary ideology to the principle of rationality now enshrined in economic solutions to the problems associated with the revolutionary situation, the centre abandoned Marxism as the guiding principle for the way ahead. Marxism died, economics became the new religion, and economists of all varieties its high priests.

At the risk of stating the obvious, I wish to set out why the shift to economics is fundamental to the current change in China: it is not a shift to any economics, but a shift from the labour theory of value to the marginal utility theory of value, and with that, a shift in a fundamental point of view towards society. The labour theory of value supposes that every component of wealth, that is, land, labour and capital, is ultimately reducible to labour. This theory was challenged towards the later years of the nineteenth century by Karl Menger and others, who argued that the value that mattered for economics was the result of utility and that alone. One difference between the labour theory of value and marginal utility is fundamental: the one sees value as intrinsic to the commodity, the other sees it as extraneous; the one is founded on the belief that labour is inherently valuable, the other that whatever the value of a commodity, there will only be a price if it is in demand; the one theory led to a theory of society in which a single motive force weighed more than any other, the other a theory in which human perception creates the categories upon which social constructs are then created. If Marxism divides society neatly into necessary classes based upon the ownership of the means of production, the thinking on which is rooted the new economics implies that society is the sum total of the means by which human action becomes calculable.[1] There is no vanguard party which of necessity must be in place to lead a predetermined proletariat. For this reason, what remains of government action has to be action justifiable by result.

Let me make clear that I am not saying that China, by discarding Marxism, is necessarily becoming capitalist. It is not clear to me that such words as socialism or capitalism are applicable to this emerging society in any absolute sense. Society is too nebulous a concept to be characterized by a single common aim. Even if we confine our concern to economic policy, if economic growth rather than ideological purity is to become a primary policy objective, the door is open for a multifarious range of means, and not all of these will be acceptable to political dogma. Once we begin to accept that the state could redistribute through taxation what it could not by ownership of the means of production, as we must after the taxation reforms in 1984, an entirely new dimension is brought into the meaning of socialism that increasingly casts fine shades between private and public ownership. How successfully the state redistributes, taking rationally into consideration the balance between immediate means and long-term ends, becomes an empirical question which will have to be examined independently from stated ideological objectives.

How any change in policy will imply social changes remains to be seen. Those of us who are more used to observing religious change than economic calculation will not be surprised that a new theology is seldom translated rapidly into religious practice, or that a remnant priesthood would not continue to purge religious differences in the name of the new creed even if not in its essence. However, in two areas at least, changes in economic policy have come together with shifts in a fundamental realignment of the relationship between community and state which will, I believe, result in some lasting features in post-revolutionary Chinese society. I refer, of course, to the responsibility system and the emergence of corporations founded on the new economics.

To explore these changes, we shall have to begin by noting how the calculability achieved through a command hierarchy is distinct from that achieved through the market, as the current Chinese economic reforms well recognize. Essentially, the rules are different: a command hierarchy works because aside from a sphere to which authority has been delegated, commands have to be obeyed, but a market works because participants are assured a sphere within which they might calculate and act in the interest of their personal benefit. The blending of the two, which forms the gist of the current economic reforms in China, requires groping for that structure in which the sphere of authority retained by the state might not interfere with the execution of choice allowed under the market. It is not easy to strike the balance. However, it is certainly not the case that a market can develop without the aid of a government bureaucracy, or that a bureaucracy can make a market economy work by intermittent and unpredictable interference.

The construction of a command hierarchy alongside a market must be distinguished from the extreme measures designed to eliminate the market that nowadays are discussed in China as "leftism", a term that suggests intensity of ideological affiliation rather than the exertion of hierarchical command. However, although it is true that the left thrived on its appeal to populism, inasmuch as popular movements had to be led and inasmuch as submission to the whims of the leader was the core content of the movements, in the unique circumstances of post-1949 China, leftism and the perpetuation of a central command were related. Looking back on the Cultural Revolution, Lynn White III has explained how those extraordinary events could have grown out of a society defined by class labels, in which periodically civil liberty could be suspended in the name of political movements declared by the party centre and executed by its branches. Selective deprivation by a centrally directed hierarchy that was unopposed by a market was a powerful tool for the exertion of a central will, and in the Cultural Revolution it was used on the party bureaucracy.[2]

The initial impact of the disturbances of the Cultural Revolution, therefore, was to destroy long-established lines of command and to engineer a realignment of loyalties. However, by the early 1970s, the movement that had begun on the claim of overturning bureaucracy was beginning to produce its own bureaucracy. An increasing number of recent studies in the West have documented this phenomenon and under different terms have come to similar conclusions. As early as 1972, Audrey Donnithorne observed that thanks to state policies that stressed self-reliance and self-sufficiency, a cellular structure had come over much of the Chinese economy.[3] Andrew Walder, who studied factory organization from the 1950s to the 1970s, noted the "indulgent patterns of authority" that emerged after work bonuses had been abolished.[4] Jean C. Oi referred to life under the cadre within collectivized agriculture as a "clientelist system".[5] Hong-yung Lee demonstrated that throughout the 1970s, the number of cadres employed in state and mass organizations increased from twelve to eighteen million.[6] Carl Riskin described the irony succinctly when he says, "Self-reliance was the default response to a lacuna in Mao's economic thought, namely, the lack of a solution to the problem of macroeconomic coordination."[7] The observation of economist Nicholas R. Lardy puts in numerical terms the consequences of strong direct control, for although net production increased between 1976 and 1980, that was more than matched by increases in input.[8] In other words, the standard of living dropped, more of what was produced went back into production, less of it was distributed.

Helen Siu, summarizing the experience of the Huancheng Commune she studied in Xinhui county, wrote of the transformation from the 1950s to the 1970s:

> The land reform destroyed the economic foundation of the lineage organizations; collectivization turned rural communities into component cells within the state sector. The communization movement incorporated the rural cadres into a tight bureaucratic network whose legitimacy was tested and strengthened through successive ideological campaigns . ... The state's presence became a major factor in the social and economic institutions of these rural communities, for it came to determine the villagers' acceptance of and resistance to the political order in which they found themselves.[9]

The general conclusion about the presence of the state applied as much to city dwellers as to villagers. Never in Chinese history was the state as powerful and as intrusive as it was from the 1950s to the 1970s.

When economic reform was declared in 1979, it was the bureaucracy that once again had to be reformed. There was common agreement that economic reform (the Four Modernizations) was of the topmost priority, but from the outset, there probably were two lines of thinking in the central leadership: China might be modernized by modernizing the bureaucracy, or it might be modernized by relaxing the bureaucracy's control on the market. Pronouncements at the end of 1978 and in 1979 appear in retrospect to be a compromise. What tipped the balance was the opening of China to outside trade, a policy that had begun from 1972 with US President Nixon's visit to China and that was confirmed and advanced in 1979 by the Chinese government's decision to permit direct investment in designated special economic zones and through joint enterprise arrangements.[10] Just as important in the short term were probably also higher prices paid for rural produce, both by the state and by the free markets that were now revived under market reforms. Prosperity was immediate in those areas where reforms came about.

In retrospect, the economic pronouncements marked the sharpest about-turn in Chinese political thinking in 1979, but to take this view we shall be guilty of forgetting that the newspaper headlines of the day were filled with revelations about the political crimes of the Gang of Four. It was not clear in 1979 and 80 that the market was to take over; what was clear was the weight that China's top leaders placed on the role of law. A major component of the discussion on law had to do with bureaucratic corruption and what came to be known as economic crime — this was the time when Liu Binyan's investigative reports gripped the popular imagination. Some effort had also to be devoted to legislation: the legal structure had fallen in the 1970s into total disarray, laws had not been drafted, and the most basic legislation was necessary. However, although legislation proceeded at a speed that surprised and impressed all observers, the limitations of a newly established legal tradition in the early years of reform are obvious. To begin with, law was to increase calculability only if the legal tradition might be considered more stable than government policy, but in the China emerging from the Cultural Revolution the two were very close. Moreover, with whatever sincerity the Chinese leadership might or might not wish to build up its law, the establishment of a legal tradition took time. Thirdly, by its very nature, law was bureaucratic, its independence being protected precisely by the establishment of its own bureaucracy. Legislation to protect investment tended to become more important in the realm of modern business corporations. In rural reform, therefore, it was not the new legislation that provided the impetus, but the responsibility system.

The responsibility system, by which term the rural reforms were referred to, was not so much a system as a revival of customary practice by default. Although the modern term *hetong* is commonly used in connection with it, it is significant that in slogans, the key word to represent the system has remained the character *bao*. It took the scholarship of the late Professor L. S. Yang, in his Qian Mu Lectures at the Chinese University of Hong Kong in 1985, to point out that the character underlies precisely the idea of contract in traditional usage.[11] To contract land from the collective and to contract for specific labour tasks are the two responsibilities for which one might "*bao*". With exactly the same term used in exactly the same way, the *Bunong shu* (Supplement to the *Book of Agriculture*) in the seventeenth century spoke of contracting for the responsibility of growing mulberry on dry land by long-term hired labourers; and in the nineteenth and the early twentieth centuries, contractors who supplied labour in factories were known as "*baogong*". The common usage of the term "*bao*" in economic relationships suggests common knowledge of the institution. This, I think, is one reason for the very rapid advance of the responsibility system after it was formally approved in 1979. Indeed, it had always been there, with or without central direction, and it had been turned to whenever the command economy had not worked. As Du Runsheng, one of the designers of the responsibility system in 1979 put it, it had surfaced four times between 1956 and 1979 without government approval, and would have surfaced again even if government had continued not to approve of it.[12]

It is now well-known that the responsibility system was introduced somewhat cautiously between 1979 and 1981. From a position in which household contracts were essentially banned, through numerous policy documents issued by the Party centre, their introduction came to be upheld as the "historical turning-point" of the party's agricultural policy. The locus classicus of the policy was the document drawn up in September 1980 by the Party centre known as "Certain problems concerning further strengthening and improvement of the responsibility system for agricultural production".[13] It is fairly well documented that although the policy was rapidly implemented, its success did not come without considerable resistance from local cadres. Yet, by December 1981 the National Agricultural Conference stated, "Up to now, over 90 percent of the production teams in the villages in the country have established different forms of agricultural responsibility systems: large-scale change has passed, the present is entering the stage of conclusion, perfection and stabilization."[14] Little did it know that this was to become a gross understatement.

Tsou Tang's conclusions on the introduction of the responsibility system in these years have probably given the most balanced attribution for the success of the system. Commenting on the situation in 1979, he noted, "Development of the system of responsibility was partly the outcome of an unorganized movement from the bottom to the top." Yet, "one should not overlook the fact that it was the top leaders who set the tone for reform and created the atmosphere."[15] This conclusion is borne out by the many local reports on the responsibility system produced in the first two years of its implementation. In the positive tone in which they are written, they indicate on the one hand the need of some central direction in overcoming local, primarily cadre, opposition to the implementation of household contracts, and on the other hand, the inability of the local leadership to stem the very creative use of contractual arrangements once they had been instituted. The opposition of local cadres was the easier problem to settle. The new programmes were well publicized, and once known, where local producers wanted responsibilities implemented, redress could be had at higher levels should they be blocked by local cadres. This is a situation that resulted from local cadres being caught between the command hierarchy that was moving towards rural reform, and a population that would have welcomed the reforms had the immediate results proved positive.

In this respect, Western field research in the provinces of Guangdong and Fujian agrees with Chinese publications. Helen Siu reports that in Huancheng Commune, Xinhui county, the local cadres held out against the responsibility system for as long as they could, families with working members that looked forward to dependence on the collective for support in old age tended to be cautious, while others, rather than taking the land they could contract from the brigade, hired out as labourers in the town.[16] Sulamith Heins Potter and Jack M. Potter noted that in Zengbu Brigade in Dongguan county, the rice harvest of 1979 was contracted out by households despite cadre opposition, and that the break with the past came really in 1980 and 1981 when "specialized contracts" (*zhuanye chengbao*) were instituted. These specialized contracts, offered through open bidding, were taken by households with greater than average resources, often because of support from relatives in Hong Kong.[17] Victor Nee, interviewing in Fujian in 1985, was also told that in 1981 cadres submitted to the responsibility system only after they had been subjected to considerable pressure.[18]

Chinese writers tended to describe in a matter-of-fact manner the introduction of written contracts in the countryside, but Western writers who examined the contracts used in these years had remarked on the similarity they bore to traditional practices. Crook's labour contract from Shaanxi struck him as being similar to a former tenancy deed, and the Potters' fishpond contract awarded on auction reminded them of economic rights that before 1949 were annually auctioned off by lineages.[19] In another respect, the privatization of work, if not property, to the household also resembled periodic bouts of commercial development in the Ming and Qing in connection with the re-emergence of free markets. The responsibility system had been introduced a year or so before rural markets were revived on a substantial scale in January 1983. The value traded in rural markets increased from 12.5 billion *yuan* in 1978 to 21.2 billion in 1980 and 38.2 billion in 1984.[20] These figures, taken with the increase in the number of *getihu*, individual household enterprises, complete the picture of the emerging rural open economy in the early 1980s. The status and rights of the individual household enterprise were guaranteed by the constitution of the People's Republic adopted by the Fifth National People's Congress in 1978 and numerous State Council policy statements published in the early 1980s.[21] The number of such rural households registered in 1981 came to a total of just short of one million, possibly an underestimate as the Association of the National Individual Household Enterprises was formed only in July 1980, but had expanded to 7 million by 1984.[22]

What has to be stressed is that although the responsibility system was designed in the first instance as an arrangement for the implementation of work contracts, once implemented, it let loose the great contractual tradition that had fuelled economic success from the Ming to the Republic with all its flexibilities. The responsibility system allowed contracts to be drawn up between individuals and collectives, leaving local arrangements to determine the varieties of purposes to which these contracts might be put. It is ironic that with or without fore-knowledge of the implications that this must have on employment, supporters of the responsibility system in 1979 to 1981 tended to propound its merits as they minimized the possibility that the success of the system would generate a class of employees. The development would have been regarded as counteractive to socialist principles. Yet, it is only necessary to follow through the immediate experience of a few cases in the application of contracts to production to see that the consequence would have been inevitable.

The following two cases cited in a paper devoted to the subject published by the Problems in Chinese Rural Development Research Group of the Chinese Academy of the Social Sciences illustrate some of these consequences:

> Case One. Zhu Jiaqing, of Fujian Province Xianyu county Longhua Commune Red Flag Brigade, member of the Chinese Communist Party, aged 49, originally head of the brigade, in 1982, teamed up with 38 households to develop hill-land by contract. Later, these householders found that it took a long time for trees to grow and the returns were small but the risk was big. They withdrew from the collective, but became hired labourers working for Zhu. They received a day's wages for a day's work, and in this way felt more secure ...

> Up to now, Zhu Jiaqing has personally invested 15,000 *yuan*, of which 6,500 *yuan* was a bank loan. In order to pay his workers' wages, repay his loan, and find the investment for 1984, he sold the sugar cane, pigs, 1,000 chickens belonging to his family, and he mortgaged two houses...

> Case Two. Liang Zouxing and Ou Fubiao of Guangdong Province Shunde county Guizhou Commune, through the connections of their relatives, in September 1982 contracted the Datan Lake of Huiyang county Donghu Commune (650 *mu* total area, 420 *mu* pond surface area) to raise fish. The contract was to last five years. For each year,

for each *mu*, he was to deliver to the commune 120 *yuan* and 15 catties of fish. The commune borrowed on behalf of the contractor 100,000 *yuan*. The contractor raised, in addition, 4,000 *yuan* for his operating expenses. After the contract [had been taken up] the Guizhou Commune of Shunde county found 11 persons to contract the management [of the pond], who were divided into 7 contracting teams. Eight fixed-term workers and 10 temporary grass-cutters were hired. (Each team kept an account of the grass it used.) Each fixed-term worker was paid 100 *yuan*. Each team was managed independently. (But putting in the fry, collecting the fish, and drawing on the funds were placed under the control of the four principal contractors Liang, Ou and others.) The Donghu Commune produced 3 commune cadres to participate (as manager of the farm, accountant and cashier). External disputes were settled by the manager of the farm. The fry were decided upon by the [principal] contractor, and the collection of money for the fish and other financial matters by the accountant and cashier designated by the commune ...[23]

The first case cited illustrates succinctly the difference between entrepreneurship and employment and shows that by choice a worker might decide to opt for one or the other. The second case illustrates the creative use of contracts to undertake, not only employment, but what would in the Western world appear rather similar to a franchise. In this rather unique series of contracts, the individual who had expertise in fish-farming provided merely the expertise, while the commune he contracted with provided funds and the pond, and the commune he originated from the labour that was subcontracted. Obviously, this arrangement had already superseded the rather simple models that were presumed when the policy was instituted in 1979, that is, of households contracting from the collective for tasks that might be fulfilled by household labour alone.

The emphasis on contracts for work, therefore, quite overshadowed a major ingredient for economic activity, the provision of capital. Yet, because of its flexibility, the responsibility system did not make it impossible for the resourceful to raise their own capital. Hence, the advantage that was gained by those households which had overseas contact, noted in studies in Guangdong and Fujian. More commonly for all parts of China, capital was to be found by resort to partnerships and shares, and those means of raising capital were only regularized by the document "On certain problems concerning present agricultural problems" issued by the Party centre in January 1983. Among the several pre-1983 references to the pooling of household resources or the use of share capital (*gufen*), in Anhui province it was reported that some households had joined together to purchase farm animals and tractors, and in Guangxi province, an operation that in 1981 had raised 11,600 *yuan* through a partnership among 11 shareholders, borrowed another 11,000 from the bank, to set up small oil refineries in adjacent villages that employed a total of 400 persons.[24] The scale of operation in private ventures was increasing, but it was not as yet a state policy to allow it to increase. As an article by Gao Kuanzhong of the Anhui University Law Faculty pointed out in 1985, the legality of household capital rested on an understanding of the household as a legal unit, and that, in turn, raised the question of whether household members ought to be considered partners in the undertaking and had implications for household formation, division and inheritance.[25] The idea of the household as a partnership would be an interesting reminder of the situation historians are now familiar with in the Ming and the Qing, when the legal household lost all touch with the conjugal unit and became a corporate body for purposes of property holding and taxation.

There were reasons to think that the revival of household contracts would, within limits, have revived the corporate structure of the lineage and the village. The crux of the matter depended, to a large extent, on the manner by which property might be held. If property must be held in the name of the corporate, then a corporate structure would have to ensue, whether it was held by households, village committees or collections of neighbouring villages. Through the 1980s, reports emerged to indicate that in places surname and neighbourhood bonds were being revived to facilitate local enterprises. Quite apart from Guangdong and Fujian, where the lineage had in pre-1949 days been given recognized prominence in the village, it was reported in an unnamed part of Hunan, that the preference for forming single-surname village committees had led to the proliferation of village committees and that lineage connections beyond the village had been revived in the interest of reclaiming grave sites.[26] In a well documented study published in 1991, village surveys in northern Jiangsu, Zhejiang, Guangdong, Guangxi, Fujian, Sichuan, Anhui, Kansu, Shaanxi, Hubei, Liaoning and Jiangxi showed, without exception, a clear recognition of kin and neighbourhood connections in village politics, an expressed revival of an interest in compiling genealogies, and in some places, a revival of lineage practices.[27] In none of the cases documented was there any indication of common property being held in the name of a lineage institution such as an ancestral hall. Nor was there any revival of the holding of property under the name of religious associations, temples or shrines. It seemed that networking took place among households, while the corporate presence in the village was firmly identified by the village and its committee.

When, by 1984, the people's commune was in effect abolished, the responsibility system was well established and attention shifted to the spectacular success of township and village enterprise. The need to regularize the new patterns of ownership that were emerging was paramount if the channelling of investment and entrepreneurial energy into rural establishments was to be continued.[28] The complications that were created by the devolution of commune and brigade activities coupled with the expansion in operational size of private enterprises are well illustrated in the following examples:

From surveys conducted by relevant departments, among the individual enterprise households in city and rural areas, "large households" that employ more than 7 persons amount to 1 percent. The largest employ more than 1,000 persons. In Taoxian *xiang* of the Dongling *cu* in Shenyang municipality, Liu, originally a brigade head, contracted for a tractor that he used for transport in 1982, made a profit every year, and his scale of operation expanded continuously. At present, he has 18 vehicles of all varieties, fixed capital of over 1 million *yuan*, and hires more than 170 persons. Besides running a transport team, he invests in 3 factories. In 1986, the profit he derived from transport alone amounted to 880,000 *yuan*. In Sanxing *xiang* of Haimen county in Jiangsu province, an individual householder has been engaged since 1979 in manufacturing garments, with a hired labour force of 24 persons in addition to putting out work to more than 80 households.

In Jiangxi province, the Guoyang Silk Dyeing and Weaving Factory was established under the initiative of and from capital raised by the factory manager Lao Yougen. It is registered as a small collective, but is in reality a private enterprise. In October 1986, its recorded staff consisted of 3,204 persons.[29]

In Wenzhou, which became an acknowledged centre of household enterprise activities, it was reported that the practice was for individual household contractors to set up their enterprises in the name of the collective.[30] In southern Jiangsu, that gained recognition as an alternative model wherein the town and village governments maintained the corporate structure in township and village enterprises, partnerships reckoned by the holding of shares became the mechanisms by which individual, collective, urban and overseas investments might together be amalgamated.[31] Township and village enterprise in southern Jiangsu had begun in the 1970s as commune and brigade industry. As Fei Xiaotong noted, it had emerged in response to the disruption in the cities brought about by the Cultural Revolution. As soon as reforms were begun in 1979, the responsibility system was applied to it as to other rural economic activities, and it had responded very rapidly to the need for capital in a vibrant market.[32] The cross-holding of shares in enterprises that came to be a feature of what around 1986 came to be known as the enterprise association (*qiye jituan*) would have had its origins in partnerships that were promoted under the rubric of township and village enterprises.

Township and village enterprises, it must be understood, included not only servicing industries in agriculture, but also, by the mid-1980s, some of China's most advanced industrial undertakings. The Stone Co., a computer manufacturer, was registered in the name of a township and village enterprise, and its revenue in 1986 amounted to 100 million *yuan*.[33] Yuhua Plastic Fans, registered in Beijiao *xiang* in Shunde county in Guangdong, which had a turnover in 1983 amounting to 8,000,000 *yuan* from the production of 50,000 electric fans, restructured its capital holdings in that year, valuing its assets at 1.4 million *yuan*, held in 14,000 shares by the commune (the commune was as yet in place), sold 2,300 shares of 100 *yuan* each in that year, and another 20,000 shares in the following year.[34] For yet another example, the *People's Daily* reported in December 1983 that the Chengguan commune in Mouping county (Shandong province) set up the following business enterprises outside the county: a restaurant in Weifang, two garment factories in far away Qiqihar and Jiamusi, and another factory to supply material for railway building in Inner Mongolia. All this was in addition to a 3-million-*yuan* investment by one of its brigades for a machine tool plant jointly set up at Mouping with a factory from Huhhot. The brigade's investment took the form of plant and land, water, electricity and labour, and the Inner Mongolian factory the expertise.[35] The mechanics of a contract of this sort can possibly be understood in terms of location. Once the economy was freed, even if only in part, locational advantages could be put to good investment use.

Nevertheless, it must be noted that under the label township and village enterprise might be found, not only advanced industries, but also the most primitive of contracts. A study of the Yantai area in Shandong conducted in 1984 estimated that 20 to 30 percent of all contracts were not fulfilled. The study was particularly critical not only of the cavalier attitude with which cadres might regard contracts, but also of the lack of legal expertise. Of 190 villages in Weihaiwei, it reported, 63 did not make use of contracts that consisted of more than one line written into the village accounting records. An example of the line was cited by the report: "One piece of orchard land at Dongshan, annual payment of 20,000; if the policy does not change, we do not change; if the policy changes, we change." Not surprisingly, the report also found that many contracts were revoked in 1984 when the Party centre extended contract terms to fifteen years. It was a constant complaint that contracting parties offered no surety for non-fulfilment of contracts (one is reminded of the fact that penalty clauses were rare in traditional Chinese contracts) while contracts revoked by the collective allowed little recourse for compensation. However, local opposition was possibly a reason for the extension of the contractual system beyond the village. That accorded with the anomaly that village operations were increasing in scale just as the law was found to be too weak for their protection.[36]

By the mid-1980s, therefore, an element of the late Qing scenario combining a vibrant market of private funds and a dearth of financial regulation on investment was beginning to be obvious. Occasionally, the situation was made quite critical by the state being periodically short of funds for its own enterprises, a situation that was found in 1984–85. The situation underlay the difference between the development of a financial market and the development of private contracts, but policy-makers did not see the problem in quite this light. Although policy-makers acknowledged the success of rural enterprises and their contribution both to increasing production and alleviating unemployment, inasmuch as investment legislation was concerned, policy-making was dominated not by the rural scene, but by the need to reform state industries.

The state industrial reforms had from 1979 been dominated by the issue of enterprise autonomy. In the first stage of these reforms, enterprises were encouraged to exceed the production quotas allotted by state agencies. Despite optimistic statistics published by Chinese sources, economists who examined the record of the reforms were not impressed by significant progress. Cyril Lin, commenting on the basis of his own interviews in 1982, was particularly acute in his criticism. "Where an enterprise was a 'profit centre' generating significant revenues for its controlling authority, the authority regarded it as a *feiruo* (tasty morsel) and was reluctant to grant it greater autonomy. Where an enterprise was a 'loss centre', the authority was eager indeed to devolve control."[37] Other writers, such as William Byrd, were more cautiously positive in arguing that the introduction of the responsibility system into enterprise management clarified the decision-making structure within enterprises.[38] All parties agreed that the introduction of the profit tax in the place of profit remittance in 1984 set a decisive change. Along with other reforms that had been taking place in the early 1980s, the net result by 1983–84 became obvious in the investment statistics of state-owned enterprises. The share of retained earnings increased from 31.9 to 43.4 percent between 1978 and 1984, budgetary grants declined from 66.4 percent to 39.0, while bank loans increased from below 1.7 percent to 15.4 percent.[39]

To speak in terms of enterprise autonomy is, of course, to speak in a half-sentence. From an early stage of enterprise reform autonomy was considered in two senses. First, it was considered in terms of the concentration of decision-making power in the hands of the factory manager. Second, it was related to the lack of horizontal linkages between enterprises, which had been aggravated by the cellular structure of the command economy. The first problem was to be solved by the introduction of the responsibility system into state enterprises, and the second was ultimately to be solved by reforming enterprise holding structures.

By 1984, it was possible for an enterprise to be contracted out to a manager on the basis of performance. The manager forming his own team had the authority to hire and fire. Yet, the introduction of the responsibility system into state enterprises did not work well. A factory was far too complex an institution to be leased to a factory manager, and if a management track record was to be a factor in the award of the lease contract, it was never clear whether productivity or profitability was to be the predominant consideration. All the while, as reiterated in the Temporary Regulations of State Enterprise issued by the State Council in April 1983, government policy required enterprises to follow policy decisions that had been set by the government agency in whose charge they were placed. Despite relaxation, many enterprises had still to abide by prices set by the state, depend on resources allocated by the state, and fulfil quotas set by the state. Moreover, as long as government policies maintained multi-tiered markets, some of that autonomy might be turned towards the exploitation of any imbalance between markets. In those circumstances, the encouragement of government bodies to form companies as a measure to encourage business activities did not always fulfil policy objectives. Relaxation in government policy, in 1979–83, 1984–85 and 1987–88, produced a large number of companies devolved from government bodies, only to be curtailed when the inflation that followed made devolution appear as a pointless squandering of public resources.[40] The application of the responsibility system in state enterprise, therefore, posed a different set of problems from its application in the rural setting.

However, the formation of new companies, the integration of existing companies, and the closure of loss-making companies was as much a central reform policy as the increased autonomy of the factory manager. In retrospect, the measures that were introduced by the Chinese government in 1986 amounted to a coherent programme to maintain control while it allowed enterprise managers greater flexibility in making their own decisions. Three measures were introduced, the bankruptcy law, enterprise associations, and cross-holding of shares by state enterprises. These various measures might have been implicit in the Seventh Five-Year Plan unveiled in April 1986, elements for which were introduced at various times in 1985. Together, they represented a considerable departure from practices advocated and followed since 1978.

A factor that must have weighed heavily in the drive towards these measures was the substantial subsidy that the state and the banking system had to pay out to state enterprises that were running at tremendous loss, and that the state deficit so brought about could not be maintained in the long term without fuelling inflation. Although legal provision for bankruptcy was a necessary consequence of enterprise autonomy in this situation, the measure was regarded as such a sharp change in fundamental socialist policies and raised so much objection that in the early years of its existence, at least, the law was only sparingly applied. The implementation of enterprise associations had a smoother history. Its gradual evolution has been documented in William A. Byrd's study of the Dongfeng Motor Vehicle Industry Associated Corporation formed originally by the Second Motor Vehicle Manufacturing Plant located in Hubei Province. When the corporation was founded in 1981, with the approval of the State Machine Building Industry Commission, it was essentially an arrangement whereby the Second Motor Vehicle Manufacturing Plant might supply truck components for assembly in eight member factories, the end products being sold under the Dongfeng label. The venture was apparently profitable to the member factories, so that as Dongfeng gained market share, the Second Motor Vehicle Manufacturing Plant could bypass state regulatory organizations and be listed as a separate line item in the state plan as early as September 1984. As Byrd remarks, "Independent status under the state plan was a rare privilege that most other enterprise groups formed in 1986–87 did not get."[41]

Byrd shows that from 1981 to 1987 the number of enterprises within the Dongfeng Corporation grew from 8 to 201. He also shows that among those member enterprises, the Second Motor Vehicle Manufacturing Plant was the leading figure: in 1984, the general manager of Dongfeng was the director of Second Motor Vehicle and only twenty members of Dongfeng headquarters staff did not simultaneously hold positions in Second Motor Vehicle. However, except for the director, top leadership posts of Dongfeng and Second Motor Vehicle were filled by different people. Less is known about financial arrangements among these different member factories at this stage. It seems clear enough that despite their membership in Dongfeng, member factories until 1987 at least retained their individual enterprise statuses. Of the 201 member factories in 1987, 162 had only what Byrd refers to as "loose" relationships with Dongfeng, defined primarily by cooperative production contracts. Presumably, these were factories that continued to assemble Dongfeng parts or that supplied parts to Dongfeng. Of the remainder, Dongfeng headquarters had the power to appoint the top executives of six member factories, and seventeen were started as joint ventures with Dongfeng after the inauguration of the Seventh Five-Year Plan. How the board of Dongfeng might have gained the authority of appointment to factories outside its immediate orbit in the days before the plan was unclear.

The history of Dongfeng illustrates well the processes whereby business corporations might adapt to the market and the speed with which the state in the 1980s recognized the necessity of reform to take this adaptation into consideration. One has to contrast enterprise models that were publicized at different times, policy statements, legal enactments, and press comments to gather a rounded picture of the coordination and conflict that must be generated by economic reforms. Policy statements prior to the end of 1985 made it explicit that enterprises entering into alliances were not to "alter the manner of the ownership arrangement, their subordination to established relationships, and their financial structure".[42] One might almost say that without some alteration of the lines of authority and financial relationships, the enterprise associations permitted up to 1985 would have been a variation of franchising, such as the assembly of truck parts under licence, the returns of which to initial capitalization might be fairly immediate. As late as November 1987, a conference called to discuss the development of enterprise associations at Second Motor Vehicle suggested, "It is necessary to specify in state policy that members of the alliance may pool capital resources, may be permitted, using as a guarantee the assets of the leading member enterprise, to raise and return loans in the name of the alliance, and to set up, with permission, finance companies and other financial institutions for regular enterprise business matters."[43]

The financing of enterprise associations could not be divorced from the question of shareholding, but that question came initially from a different context. Shares were known from the early days of economic reform in the early 1980s. Surely, the holding of shares could not but be a part of the responsibility system, and it was an essential part of Sino-foreign joint-ventures. The issuing of shares by private enterprise was given some publicity from 1984, and the subject had been brought in every now and then in relation to state enterprises up to that time. However, the cross-holding of shares by state enterprises did not begin until 1986, first among various local enterprises in Shenyang, where the Bankruptcy Law was being introduced.[44] Some confusion must have existed between such cross-holding of shares by enterprises and the issuing of shares to the public by private companies, for in March 1987 the State Council directed that no state enterprise was to issue shares to the public unless permission had been given by the People's Bank, exempting from this rule all those share issues that had already been offered.[45] From 1988, it would seem that the cross-holding of shares was a regular instrument in the establishment of enterprise associations, and the State Enterprise Law of that year clearly legalized such arrangements.

Several articles published in the *People's Daily* in 1986 explaining the ideological correctness of share offers from state enterprises laid out quite clearly the thinking behind this policy shift. Tong Dalin argued essentially that what made shareholding socialist in the arrangement it had been given in China was that the major shareholders were the enterprises and their workers. Li Yining went further, considering less the ideological import of the payment of dividends by the enterprise than the question of enterprise control via shareholding. He pointed out that in the event that a holding structure was in place, the state could maintain an effective voice on the board of directors without perhaps more than a third of the overall holding capital. Moreover, because each subsidiary company within the holding structure was independently managed but accountable to the parent company, the structure permitted "the union of centralization and devolution".[46] One may be forgiven to read in this the discovery that the capitalist had all along had the better means of enterprise control. Why, indeed, insist of 100 percent ownership when a fraction of this would do?

With the cross-holding of shares, incorporation as a process whereby an autonomous business structure might be brought into existence was once again in place. This time around, there were good reasons to resort to these measures. The combination of cross-holding of shares and the enterprise association, far from allowing the state to maintain control, had allowed the corporation to take off. This was possible because of one unforeseen consequence of these various measures, that is, internal banking. Essentially, the legal framework allowed state enterprises to rationalize, to hive off areas that were unprofitable, and as long as capital was available, to regroup those sections that were profitable into a viable holding structure. The question may well be asked where all the capital that might be needed for rationalization was to come from. The answer is not hard to find. After the machinery for rationalization had been put in place by 1988, and a clear signal of party centre support was given in Deng Xiaoping's visit to Shenzhen in 1992, the Hang Seng index in Hong Kong doubled. The regulations for the reorganization of state enterprise promulgated by the State Council in 1992, following on from the State Enterprise Law of 1988, had made it amply clear that practically all of China's state enterprise was due for rationalization. More than 2,000 conglomerates came into existence within those few

years, many with partners or subsidiaries in Hong Kong. The price
of listed stock on the Hong Kong market appreciated because, in a
very real sense, the assets of Hong Kong's listed companies had
grown, thanks to opportunities which became available of expansion
in China through mergers.

Towards the end of the 1980s, China's encounter with capitalism
had reached a new stage. The command economy had been all but
replaced by the autonomous, if not always private, corporation. In a
sense, it had gone full circle back to the late Qing, when the modern
company was brought into being, via the privatization of central and
local government monopolies and the transformation of the family
into the firm.

A Postscript

In updating the above in 1994 I cited some comments made then by
experienced practitioners in the China field which noted the
persistence of family control in Chinese business. Mr (later Sir)
Gordon Wu, a reputable engineer and real estate developer, in an
address to the BOT ("Build, operate and transfer") Asia '94
Conference on the subject of the execution of BOT projects, said:

> Always show preference for a local player but do not be surprised if
> the local player is related to the first family or there is some other
> political consideration.[47]

And Mr Lawrence Weinbach, chief executive of international
accounting firm, Arthur Anderson:

> In operations and corporate strategy, Hong Kong and mainland [PRC]
> companies were similar in structure and outlook to those found in the
> West. What was different in Asia was the role of the controlling
> shareholders, often a family, or leading figure in the group ... Asian
> companies tended to stress the roles of these parties while in the West
> the roles of the board and independent shareholders were more
> developed.[48]

Hong Kong moving towards reversion to Chinese sovereignty then was concerned with the question of corruption and bribery in China's business culture. Under the heading, "Conflicts of interest not so easy to resolve", the *South China Morning Post* summarized a growing debate that had arisen out of reports independently published by two of Hong Kong's public bodies, the Hong Kong government's Independent Commission Against Corruption (ICAC) and the Hong Kong Stock Exchange. The ICAC had conducted a survey and come to the conclusion that conflicts of interest were a cause of corruption complaints, while the Hong Kong Stock Exchange had produced a discussion document which suggested that the exchange should reduce its regulatory role on the accuracy of company reports. The *South China Morning Post*'s reporter drew from the two documents the following conclusion:

> Hong Kong's traditional business methods are coming under pressure. How the established family firm, with its spider's web of connections, cross holdings and filial loyalties, fits in with modern methods of commerce and regulation is under the microscope ... The two subjects are linked because the close connections that many listed companies have with the extra family interests of their directors often raise the possibility of conflicts of interest.[49]

In 1994, these were ominous words. By 1997, when the Asian financial crisis set in, family connections and patronage came to be referred to as "cronyism".

The persistence of the Chinese family firm and family control of modern Chinese corporations in Hong Kong is well-known. Looking at these reports in the light of the long-term development of Chinese business practices, I think they fit in with the impression, in Chinese business history, of the conflict between private contract and the investment market. The culture fostered by the two is so very different that one might think of them as belonging to two different worlds.

The world of the private contract survives on the institutions of patronage. Parties to the contract pronounce that they abide by personal trust, and they make contracts which are no more than statements of intent. No penalty clause is included because, in the absence of an independent means of enforcing the contract, a penalty clause does not serve a lot of purpose. In the event that the contract leads to disputes, signatories appeal to their connections, who would often be their patrons, to resolve their disputes. When the patrons fail, diplomacy fails, and depending on circumstances the failure may lead to outright warfare. In this world, trust is a personal attribute.

In the world of high finance, investors seek a market in which finance houses offer service in competition for a fee. In order to compete, those institutions not only advertise their success in terms of higher dividends paid than their competitors, but they also project the image that they can be in charge even in a volatile climate because their knowledge of the financial market gives them an edge over uncertainty. They stress their ability to calculate, and hence to maximize. Towards this end, they demand openness and accountability from the institutions that they invest in. While they may stress detailed knowledge of these institutions, including their personnel, they do not, in their advertising, expose themselves to arbitrary decisions that may rest on the personal preferences of chief executives. In this world, calculability is institutional.

Let me not sound over-optimistic. The argument presented here is *not* that patronage is absent in the legally binding capital market, or that institutional, rather than personal, expectations need be absent when contracts are concluded in secrecy and accounts are never published. Nor is it that with changes in law, the players' attitudes in the highly dramatic stages of the business theatre might change overnight. The question being raised through an examination of the history of paper instruments and incorporation in Chinese business is how trust can be transferred. Trust resting in the person is not readily transferable; the paper instrument may be; the incorporation which rests on patronage is not open to governance, that which recognizes the rights of the investor has to be. The transferability of the paper instrument and the openness required of the modern corporation made possible the stock market. The result is the possibility of expressing institutional calculability in the value of transferable shares. The conditions which make the share transferable, that is to say, requirements imposed on company incorporation, the existence of stock exchanges, and clearly stated rules on transaction, do not exclude personal trust in the capital market. They seek to bar the circulation of information among people who maintain trust in private in order to exclude access to the wider public. This business structure is designed to allow capital to circulate, while in contrast, the business structure built upon personal trust is not one in which capital can readily circulate. The principles of capitalism cannot go very far in the business structure that rests alone on personal trust.

In light of my expectation that a change in the business culture must precede the erosion of patronage, I think it is highly significant that in the last decades, especially since the Accounting Law of 1993, the Chinese firm has been rapidly moving towards greater institutional openness.[50] Two Chinese authors adding up the publications in accounting in recent years noted 261 items from 1949 to 1959, 173 from 1960 to 1979, 280 for the five years of 1980 to 1984, 1,266 in the following five years of 1985 to 1989, and 1,312 from 1990 to 1997. The Chinese Institute of Certified Public Accountants, founded in 1995, noted that at the end of 2002, China had 60,000 certified public accountants who were practising and 70,000 non-practising.[51] The tremendous interest in accounting is duplicated in management and business, where enrolment in tertiary education leaped from 12,000 in 1980 to 67,000 in 1991, and engineering, from 92,000 in 1980 to 214,000 in 1991.[52] The numbers speak of increasing professionalization, which in the field of accounting, has been moving in the direction, not only of the application of accounts to management but also to independent auditing. The world of investment in the West knows only too well that no amount of audit control demolishes miscalculation and fraud, but without the formal institution of accounting and law, no governance of public ownership would have been possible. And more, the discussion on governance as accounting and law are instituted makes an impact on perception, behaviour and standards. This last is again easy to misrepresent: I am not being naive to the extent that I would imagine that what the law requires, businesses perform. I refer to a change in the business environment which must come if share capital is to make an impact on business investment. This is the change in business attitude necessitated by the professionalization of the capital market, when investors with small amounts of capital pool their resources in investment funds of various sorts. Fund managers not only need to calculate risk, but also to be seen to be able to calculate risk, and the investor has to be educated to seek out fund managers who perform.[53] That is the change from making investments using one's own capital, to making investment with other people's capital, which is, after all, what the relatively recent phenomenon of the finance industry is all about.

In summary, my argument in these chapters has been that the institutions supported by private contracts, that is, contracts between individuals or groups without reference to or support from the state, were given considerable room to develop from the sixteenth century. By the nineteenth century, Chinese people high and low, men and women, were experts in the use of private contracts. However, China was backward in the realm of financing capital-intensive projects. The institutions for financing such projects could not have been advanced without the support of the state and without the state being prepared to give way to the market. On two occasions before 1949, China had made only false starts along the course that might have produced industrial banking on a scale that would have supported modern industry. In the 1980s, it made its third attempt and, while writing in the 1990s, I was still saying we had to wait to see how far those efforts would go. Writing now in the early years of the twenty-first century, it is hard to see that China can turn the clock back, but this is not to say that the standards advocated by law would be adopted all over China. In many parts of China, the culture of the finance market has still to battle it out with the culture of patronage, but the more it is seen that the middling investor needs the protection of law if he or she is to invest, the more patronage will have to give way to transparency.

6 Conclusion

This broad sweep of the business history of China highlights the following aspects of traditional Chinese business institutions:

- Written contracts relating to land were commonly employed.
- Chinese corporations emerged from a ritual context.
- Patronage took paramount importance in all businesses, and political patronage in businesses of scale.
- Traditional Chinese accounting lacked the means to calculate capital.
- The transformation of Chinese institutions from the nineteenth to the twentieth century required the adaptation of business to commercial law.
- Traditional business was limited to knowledge of capital within the group, and the legal basis for business institutionalized transparency in corporate governance.

This is not meant to be an exhaustive list. It is a list that is arrived at by positing contracts, accounting, incorporation, and financing as major elements of business. In the process, I have related these features of Chinese business to the sixteenth-century commercial revolution, when the lineage as a corporation came into its own and when the sale of salt tickets collapsed and with that, the end of any chance for the evolution of a capital market. China did not follow the course of events which the Western world went through: no law guaranteeing individual ownership of property was instituted, but instead, the practice of holding properties in the names of ancestors and deities became paramount. As long as business enterprise required limited capitalization, the ritual institutions were sufficient for the task of raising capital. The shortfall came when nineteenth-century industry, introduced by the West, called for investments on unprecedented scales in the Chinese experience. Chinese institutions were unable to rise to the need.

Major changes were made to this manner of business by the last decades of the nineteenth century, many of which were associated with the erosion of China's political sovereignty under the threat of war and political turmoil. From the last years of the nineteenth century to the whole of the twentieth century, it may be said that:

- Chinese firms increasingly took on the character of companies as defined in successive versions of the Company Law.
- Banks remained the weakest link in the business chain but signs may be detected of an impact being made by banking practices.
- Since the 1930s accounting has evolved as a profession but the enforcement of accountability has not yet been settled.
- Families continued to wield power within the framework of the public company.
- Patronage remained a requirement in the world of business.

Some of these features can be traced to legislation and its enforcement in China proper and in areas where Chinese businesses proliferate. Some features have continued not because of any tenacity of tradition but because twentieth century governments have adopted policies similar to their nineteenth-century predecessors. The finance market has wielded a much stronger impact on the practice of businesses, but the jury is still out as to whether Chinese firms might be made accountable to their shareholders to the same degree as Western firms might be. In none of these changes did Confucianism as an ideology have any bearing.

I have little to quarrel with Kenneth Pomeranz in searching for a "great divergence" with the West to elucidate China's experience in economic development. He has a point in locating some of that in the control of the oceans by the West. Yet, I would describe the divergence in very different terms. I think he has brushed aside too summarily the differences in the business institutions of China and the West, in particular, the manner by which corporations might be founded and maintained. Or, in other words, were property to be held by a group, rather than an individual, how it might be held.

It goes without saying that the process of incorporation holds a central place in the history of business. Were comparison to be made with the Western European and North American experience, the history of business incorporation would embrace the history of partnerships, the chartered companies, the banks, limited liability, shareholding, credit-bearing instruments (commercial papers, in the form of drafts and bills), paper currencies, public debt, and associated with these practices, the emergence of commercial law and standard accounting practices. It is true that a great deal of this development came within the nineteenth and twentieth centuries, and the point of comparison, were it to contribute to an explanation of divergence in economic growth, would have to pertain to the eighteenth century. It is also true that the history of many of these institutions in China is a great deal hazier than it is in Europe and North America, not only because historical documentation has been in short supply, but also because the Chinese experience has not been told in institutional terms.

In brief, it can be said of Chinese business history that China underwent a commercial revolution, very much as Western Europe did, in the sixteenth century. Out of the commercial revolution, business traditions developed which incorporated many instruments which serviced trade and investment. Contracts were commonly used, many of them written even though many more must have remained oral. Partnerships were formed. Moreover, even though membership to corporations did not go very far beyond circles of relatives and acquaintances, property was held in the name of the group as a body and maintained an independent existence beyond the lifetimes of the individuals who might make up the group. However, despite these similarities with the West, eighteenth-century China did not have as much as a nascent stock market nor did its government acquire a national debt. For that reason, China did not have banks which were experienced in dealing with a national debt or paper currencies issued on that basis. These similarities and differences are vital in the explanation of China's divergence from the West by the time of the iron-and-steel industrial revolution. Chinese people continued to excel in commerce where small groups of merchants networked through friends and family, but came to grieve in capital-intensive enterprises such as running steamships, mines and railways.

Pomeranz is correct, therefore, to draw attention away from the ubiquitous reference to "culture" in the China literature towards institutional differences. Yet, the concept of cultural differences — not necessarily a Confucian East pitched against a Christian West — must creep back in the comparative context. After all, a comparative study is only meaningful when history is not regarded as a descriptive course of events, but as a series of twists and turns all of which could have led to alternative courses of development. What might have happened if the Ming emperors had been more successful in building up a national debt denominated in salt? Probably not enough of a background to allow any reasonable conjecture that it would lead to the beginnings of a paper currency backed by a reserve. But what if the kings of England in the first half of the seventeenth century were as powerful as the Ming emperors and might abrogate their debts? There would not have been a Bank of England. The national debt founded on salt tickets proved to be a blind alley, and so the Ming government, and the Qing government to follow it, took the course of "government supervision and merchant management", euphemism for business under political patronage.

If the capitalist road of the salt ticket proved a dead end, not so the other institutions for trade and investment from the sixteenth-century commercial revolution. Here, again, some details are needed for the difference between China and the West to be understood. The corporations which served as the instruments of investment in eighteenth-century China had long been known to China historians but few had recognized in them the economic vehicles which they had become. Unlike Western Europe, where by the eighteenth century business incorporation was increasingly governed by a law with the explicit recognition that gaining a profit was rightful and legal, eighteenth-century Chinese corporations remained ritual entities, established not directly to serve the interests of their members, but ostensibly to provide sacrifice for gods and ancestors. Compared to Europe, the Chinese corporation would have been akin to the medieval monastery, built for a religious purpose but maintained as a powerhouse of economic growth, managing land and hostels, providing services — not without charge — for living and dead, and networking with kings and peasants. The analogy creates its own problems, of course, there being no church in China equivalent to the religious establishment of Western society, the very diversified and decentralized corporate entities which might be established around shrines and temples answered to no clergy. Through the Ming and the Qing dynasties, authority of interpretation as to what might or might not be proper behaviour at shrines and temples was claimed, not by the religious specialists, who might be thought of as village shamans, Buddhist monks and Daoist priests, but by the literati schooled in the Confucian classics.

The comparison with Europe necessarily breaks down, as the description of Chinese society skirts nearer the much publicized East Asian tenet to what counts as a unique culture under the name "Confucianism". It would be necessary to strip of that idea any reference to Confucius, or any inkling that the ideology pervaded society to such an extent that it competed with "Daoism" or "Buddhism". The moral tenets it advocated as an ideology were translated into action only to the extent that moral tenets might. It downgraded mercantile activities, but that is not to say that the governments of the time did not recognize the value of trade or that society was not pervaded by the pursuit of profit. Left standing would be the close identification of the local to the central in terms of a common ritual, the separation of the emperor's personal religious faith from the religious rituals of the state, a four-century-long trend of upward social mobility demarcated by the acquisition of official status by examination and the production of a literati class which saw its fortunes closely entwined with its defence of state orthodoxy. This was the society which rested its order on ritual rather than law, which recognized group rather than individual responsibility, and which legitimized official patronage rather than legal rights in business. Call this "culture" if one must, for embedded in it were beliefs and social practices which did set China off from the West.

More than the oceans and the inner Asian deserts separated China from the West. East and West diverged in the innovations each brought to the common problem of harnessing resources in the drive for wealth and power. It falls to the historian to identify the trajectories on which these innovations were set, and, thereby, provide an understanding for the varied experience of the very large numbers of people living on the opposite sides of the world.

Notes

Chapter 1

1 Xu Dixin and Wu Chengming, *Zhongguo ziben zhuyi fazhan shi* (A history of the development of capitalism in China), Beijing: Renmin chubanshe, 1985–1993, 3 volumes, of which volume 1 is available in English translation as Xu Dixin and Wu Chengming, eds. *Chinese Capitalism, 1522–1840*, Basingstoke: Macmillan, 2000; Ma Min and Zhu Ying, *Chuantong yu jindai de erchong bianzou: wan Qing Suzhou shanghui gean yanjiu* (Duet of tradition and modernity: A case study of the Suzhou Chamber of Commerce in the late Qing), Chengdu: Bashu shushe, 1993, and Ma Min, *Guanshang zhi jian: shehui jubian zhong de jindai shenshang* (Between the merchant and the official: The gentry merchant in a time of momentous social change), Tianjin: Tianjin renmin, 1995. Ma Min's argument may be found in English summary in Ma Min, "Emergent civil society in the late Qing dynasty: The case of Suzhou", in David Faure and Tao Tao Liu, eds. *Town and Country in China: Identity and Perception*, Basingstoke: Palgrave, 2002, pp. 145–65.

2 Among the exceptions must be included: Thomas G. Rawski, *Economic Growth in Prewar China*, Berkeley: University of California Press, 1989; Thomas G. Rawski and Lillian M. Li, eds. *Chinese History in Economic Perspective*, Berkeley: University of California Press, 1992; Sherman Cochran, *Big Business in China: Sino-foreign Rivalry in the Cigarette Industry, 1890–1930*, Cambridge, MA: Harvard University Press, 1990; *Encountering Chinese Networks: Western, Japanese, and Chinese Corporations in China, 1880–1937*, Berkeley: University of California Press, 2000; Ramon Myers, *The Chinese Peasant Economy: Agricultural Development in Hopei and Shantung, 1890–1949*, Cambridge, MA: Harvard University Press, 1970; and Albert Feuerwerker, *China's Early Industrialization, Sheng Hsuan-huai (1844–1916) and Mandarin Enterprise*, New York: Atheneum 1970 (first ed. 1958).

3 Guo Daoyang, *Zhongguo kuaiji shi gao* (A history of Chinese accounting), Beijing: Zhongguo caizheng jingji chubanshe, 1982, 1988; and Gao Zhiyu, *Zhongguo kuaiji fazhan jianshi* (A concise history of Chinese accounting), Henan renmin chubanshe, 1985.

4   For some background on this argument, see Etienne Balazs, *Chinese Civilization and Bureaucracy: Variations on a Theme*, transl. and edited by Arthur F. Wright, New Haven: Yale University Press, 1964; and Lloyd E. Eastman, *Family, Fields, and Ancestors, Constancy and Change in China's Social and Economic History, 1550–1949*, Oxford: Oxford University Press, 1988.

5   Mary Clabaugh Wright, ed. *China in Revolution: The First Phase, 1900–1913*, New Haven: Yale University Press, 1968.

6   For description of social and political changes in the Republican period, see Henrietta Harrison, *The Making of the Republican Citizen: Political Ceremonies and Symbols in China 1911–1929*, Oxford: Oxford University Press, 2000, and John Fitzgerald, *Awakening China: Politics, Culture, and Class in the Nationalist Revolution*, Stanford: Stanford University Press, 1996.

7   Background of policy changes in the late 1970s and 1980s may be found in Joseph Fewsmith, *Dilemmas of Reform in China: Political Conflict and Economic Debate*, Armonk, NY: M. E. Sharpe, 1994; *China's Second Revolution: Reform after Mao*, Washington, DC: Brookings Institution, c. 1987.

Chapter 2

1   Andre Gunder Frank, *Reorient: Global Economy in the Asian Age*, Berkeley, London: University of California Press, 1998; Kenneth Pomeranz, *The Great Divergence: China, Europe, and the Making of the Modern World Economy*, Princeton: Princeton University Press, 2000.

2   J. Y. Wong, *Deadly Dreams, Opium and the Arrow War (1856–1860) in China*, Cambridge: Cambridge University Press, 1998, pp. 337–60.

3   Raymond Dawson, *The Chinese Chameleon: An Analysis of European Conceptions of Chinese Civilization*, London: Oxford University Press, 1967.

4   On this interpretation of the classical economics background to *Capital*, see Louis Dumont, *From Mandeville to Marx: The Genesis and Triumph of Economic Ideology*, Chicago: University of Chicago Press, 1977.

5   Max Weber, *Economy and Society: An Outline of Interpretive Sociology*, Berkeley: University of California Press, 1978; Karl Polanyi, *The Great Transformation: The Political and Economic Origins of Our Time*, Boston: Beacon Press, 1957; Fernand Braudel, *Civilization and Capitalism 15th–18th Century*, transl. by Sian Reynolds, London: Collins, 1981.

6   The word "lineage" is used in Chinese social history to refer to groups of people of the same surname tracing ancestry from a common ancestor.

7 For some of these thoughts in the eighteenth century, see Helen Dunstan, *Conflicting Counsels to Confuse the Age: A Documentary Study of Political Economy in Qing China, 1644–1840*, Ann Arbor: Centre for Chinese Studies, University of Michigan, 1996.

8 The recognition of the independence of the market, and the connection between the price of silver and the export of opium is exemplified in Bao Shichen, "Gengchen zazhu" (Miscellaneous writings of the year Gengzhen, that is, 1820), especially item 2, reprinted in Zhao Jing and Yi Menghong eds. *Zhongguo jindai jingji sixiang ziliao xuanji*, Beijing: Xinhua, 1982, *shang*, pp. 8–13. The politics of the group of senior officials with whom Bao was associated and its connections to the outbreak of the Opium War is discussed in James M. Polachek, *The Inner Opium War*, Cambridge, MA: Council on East Asian Studies, Harvard University, 1992.

9 Karl Marx, *Capital: A Critical Analysis of Capitalist Productions*, London: William Glaisher Ltd., 1920, p. 103, n. 1; Wu Han, "Wang Maoyin yu Xianfeng shidai de huobi gaige" (Wang Maoyin and the currency reform in Xianfeng), *Zhongguo shehui jingjishi jikan*, 1937, reprinted in Wu Han, *Dushi zhaji*, Beijing: Sanlian, 1956, pp. 65–91; and Wang's memorials in Zhao Jing, Yi Menghong, *Zhongguo jindai jingji sixiang ziliao xuanji*, pp. 363–80.

10 For a similar view expressed by Chinese historians, see Han Dacheng, "Mingdai shangpin jingji de fazhan yu ziben zhuyi de mengya" (The development of the commodity economy in the Ming dynasty and the sprouts of capitalism), in Zhongguo renmin daxue Zhongguo lishi jiaoyanshi, ed. *Ming-Qing shehui jingji xingtai de yanjiu* (Studies in the social and economic structures of the Ming and the Qing), Shanghai: Shanghai renmin, 1957, pp. 1–102.

11 Susan Naquin and Evelyn S. Rawski, *Chinese Society in the Eighteenth Century*, New Haven: Yale University Press, 1987.

12 The locus classicus of the "sprouts of capitalism" argument remains Shang Yue, *Zhongguo ziben zhuyi guanxi fasheng ji yanbian de chubu yanjiu* (Preliminary studies of the origins and development of Chinese capitalist relationships), Beijing: Sanlian, 1956, which may be supplemented by the papers incorporated into Zhongguo renmin daxue Zhongguo lishi jiaoyanshi, ed. *Zhongguo ziben zhuyi mengya wenti taolunji* (Discussions on the question of the sprouts of capitalism in China), Beijing: Sanlian, 1957, and Nanjing daxue lishixi Zhongguo gudaishi jiaoyanshi, ed. *Zhongguo ziben zhuyi mengya wenti taolunji, xubian* (Discussions on the question of the sprouts of capitalism in China, supplementary volume), Beijing: Sanlian, 1960. An ideological criticism of Shang Yue's argument

may be found in Liu Danian, "Guanyu Shang Yue tongzhi wei *Ming-Qing shehui jingji xingtai de yanjiu* yishu suoxie de xuyan" (On the preface written by comrade Shang Yue for the book *Studies in the Social and Economic Structures of the Ming and the Qing*), *Lishi yanjiu*, 1958:1, reprinted in Nanjing daxue lishixi Zhongguo gudaishi jiaoyanshi, ed. *Zhongguo ziben zhuyi mengya wenti taolunji, xubian*, pp. 306–30. Much of the research on the theme has been incorporated into Xu Dixin and Wu Chengming, *Zhongguo Ziben zhuyi fazhan shi.*

13   Fu Zhufu, "Youguan ziben zhuyi mengya de jige wenti" (Concerning several questions on the sprouts of capitalism), in Fu Zhufu, *Zhongguo jingjishi luncong*, Beijing: Sanlian, 1980, pp. 669–708.

14   Sidney Pollard, *The Genesis of Modern Management: A Study of the Industrial Revolution in Great Britain*, Harmondsworth: Penguin, 1968.

15   Peng Zeyi, "Cong Mingdai guanying zhizao de jingying fangshi kan Jiangnan sizhiye shengchan de xingzhi" (A view of the nature of Jiangnan silk production from the Ming official silk works), *Lishi yanjiu*, 1963:2, reprinted in Cuncui xueshe, *Zhongguo jin sanbai nian shehui jinjishi lunji*, vol. 3, Hong Kong: Cuncui xueshe, 1979, pp. 46–69; Peng Zeyi, "Qingdai qianqi Jiangnan zhizao de yanjiu" (A study of the Jiangnan silk workshops in the early Qing), *Lishi yanjiu*, 1963:4, in Cuncui xueshe, *Zhongguo jin sanbai nian*, vol. 2, pp. 79–104; Paolo Santangelo, "The imperial factories of Suzhou: Limits and characteristics of state intervention during the Ming and Qing dynasties", in S. R. Schram, ed. *The Scope of State Power in China*, London and Hong Kong: School of Oriental and African Studies and Chinese University Press, 1985, pp. 269–94.

16   Documentation may be found in Deng Tuo, "Cong Wanli dao Qianlong, guanyu Zhongguo ziben zhuyi mengya shiqi de yige lunzheng" (From Wanli to Qianlong, an item of evidence on the period of the sprouts of capitalism in China), in *Lishi yanjiu*, 1956, October, reprinted in Nanjing daxue lishixi, *Zhongguo ziben zhuyi mengya, xubian*, pp. 133–82; Hu Tiewen, "Shilun Qing qianqi Jingde zhen zhiciye zhong guanyao, hanghui tong ziben zhuyi mengya de guanxi" (A tentative argument on the connections of official kilns and guilds in the porcelain industry at Jingde *zhen* to the sprouts of capitalism in the early Qing), *Zhongguo shehui kexueyuan jingji yanjiusuo jikan*, vol. 5, 1983, pp. 205–24. The two account books discussed in Liang Miaotai, "Qingdai Jingde zhen yichu lucun yaohao de shouzhi yingli" (Profit derived from income and expenditure at a certain *lucun* kiln in Jingde *zhen* in the Qing period); *Zhongguo shehui jingjishi yanjiu*, 1984: 4, pp. 1–16, are also highly relevant to the issue here. One of these two appears to be a journal of daily expenses, that include such items as fuel, food for workmen, watchmen's

fees, and donations, perhaps mandatory, to charities. It is significant that although this book would indicate that items of production expenses were recorded, there was no apparent attempt to analyse them. Presumably the accounts where kept so that a total expenditure might be deducted from total income derived from a separate book. In that case, it should be clear that the object of keeping these books was not so much an attempt to understand production costs as to provide a basis for working out the profit balance. For continuation of sub-contracting into the twentieth century, see also Elisabeth Koll, *From Cotton Mill to Business Empire: The Emergence of Regional Enterprises in Modern China*, Cambridge, MA: Harvard University Press, 2004, pp. 81–119, and Tim Wright, "A method of evading management — contract labour in Chinese coal mines before 1937", in Rajeswary Ampalavanar Brown, *Chinese Business Enterprise*, New York: Routledge, 1996, vol. 3, pp. 505–27.

17 Peng Zeyi, "Qingdai Baoquan Baoyuan ju yu zhuqian gongye" (The Baoquan and Baoyuan Offices and the coin-minting industry in the Qing), *Zhongguo shehui kexueyuan jingji yanjiusuo jikan*, vol. 5, 1983, pp. 179–204.

18 Lu Shuyi, "Zhongguo jindai de gongcang guanli yu laogong wenti — Zhongguo jindai gongcang li de laogong chaowu, jianguan zhidu yu Zhongguo laogong yundong" (Modern Chinese factory management and the labour problem — labour recruitment and supervision and the Chinese labour movement), unpublished MA dissertation, Chinese University of Hong Kong, 1984, pp. 97–118.

19 Geoffrey Parker, "The emergence of modern finance in Europe, 1500–1730", Carlo M. Cipolla, ed. *The Fontana Economic History of Europe, the Sixteenth and Seventeenth Centuries*, London: Fontana/Collins, 1974, pp. 527–94.

20 David Faure, "What made Foshan a town? The evolution of rural-urban identities in Ming-Qing China", *Late Imperial China*, 11:2, 1990, pp. 1–31.

21 William T. Rowe, referring to his study of the eighteenth-century official, Chen Hongmou, wrote, "There can be no question that Chen and his contemporaries did not operate with anything like the construction of the 'individual' that found favour in the early modern West. Certainly, the 'individual' was not for them the locus of proprietorship. That locus was the family, and not just any family, but rather the highly particularized, multigenerational, Chinese-style family prescribed by the Confucian canon." William T. Rowe, "Economics and culture in eighteenth-century China", Kenneth G. Lieberthal, Shuen-fu Lin and Ernest P. Young, eds. *Constructing China: The Interaction of Culture and Economics*, Ann Arbor: Centre for Chinese Studies, University of Michigan, 1997, p. 17.

22   The recent debate on civil society in Chinese history is relevant to this issue. See Frederic Wakeman, "The civil society and public sphere debate: Western reflections on Chinese political culture", *Modern China*, 19:2, 1993, pp. 108–38, and William T. Rowe, "The problem of 'civil society' in late imperial China", *Modern China*, 19:2, 1993, pp. 139–57. On patronage, see also Prasenjit Duara, *Culture, Power and the State, Rural North China, 1900–1942*, Stanford: Stanford University Press, 1988, p. 183.

23   Arthur H. Smith, *Village Life in China: A Study in Sociology*, Edinburgh: Oliphant, Anderson and Ferrier, 1900, pp. 49–53, 141–60; Fei Hsiao-tung, *Peasant Life in China: A Field Study of Country Life in the Yangtze Valley*, London: Routledge and Kegan Paul, 1939, pp. 240–63; G. William Skinner, "Marketing and social structure in rural China", *Journal of Asian Studies*, 24:1, 1964, pp. 3–43; 24:2, 1965, pp. 195–228; and 24:3, 1965, pp. 363–99.

24   Liang Jiabin, *Guangdong shisanhang kao* (A study of the thirteen *hang* of Guangdong), Shanghai: Guoli bianyiguan, 1937; Fu Yiling, *Ming-Qing shidai shangren ji shangye ziben* (Merchants and merchant capital in the Ming and the Qing periods), Beijing: Renmin, 1956.

25   Wei Qingyuan, "Lun Qingdai de huangdang", (A study of the imperial pawnshops of the Qing period), and "Lun Qingdai de diandangye yu guanliao ziben" (A study of the pawn-broking business and official capital in the Qing period), in Wei Qingyuan, *Ming-Qing shi bianxi*, Beijing: Zhongguo shehui kexue, 1989, pp. 70–112 and 128–65.

26   Wei Qingyuan, "Qingdai Kangxi shiqi 'shengxi yinliang' zhidu de chuchuang he yunyong" (The origin and operation of the system of 'silver invested for interest' in the Kangxi period in the Qing); "Qingdai Yongzheng shiqi 'shengxi yinliang' zhidu de zhengdun he zhengce yanbian" (The reorganization of and policy changes in the system of 'silver invested for interest' in the Yongzheng period in the Qing); "Qingdai Qianlong shiqi 'shengxi yinliang' zhidu de shuaibai he 'shouche' " (The decline and 'withdrawal' of the system of 'silver invested for interest' in the Qianlong period in the Qing), in Wei Qingyuan, *Ming-Qing shi bianxi*, pp. 166–85, 186–228, and 229–56.

27   Andrea Lee McElderry, *Shanghai Old-style Banks (ch'ien-chuang) 1800–1935*, Ann Arbor: Centre for Chinese Studies, University of Michigan, 1976, pp. 105–29.

28   There is a substantial literature on the Huizhou merchants, of which the following are possibly the most comprehensive treatments: Fujii Hiroshi, "Xin'an shangren de yanjiu" (A study of the Xin'an merchants, translated from Japanese), in *Jianghuai luntan* bianjibu, eds. *Huishang yanjiu lunwenji*, Hefei: Anhui renmin, 1985, pp. 131–269; Ye Xianen, *Ming-Qing Huizhou nongcun shehui yu dianbuzhi* (Rural society and the

system of bonded tenants in Huizhou in the Ming and Qing), Hefei: Anhui renmin, 1983; and Harriet Zurndorfer, *Change and Continuity in Chinese Local History: The Development of Hui-chou Prefecture 800 to 1800,* The Hague: E. J. Brill, 1989.

29 Xu Hong, "Mingdai qianqi de shiyan yunxiao zhidu" (Arrangements for the transport and sale of edible salt in the early Ming), *Taiwan daxue wenshizhe xuebao* 23, 1974, pp. 221–66; Ray Huang, *Taxation and Government Finance in Sixteenth-Century Ming China*, Cambridge: Cambridge University Press, 1974, pp. 189–224.

30 Ma Yinchu, *Zhonghua yinhang lun* (A treatise on Chinese banking), Shanghai: Shangwu, 1929.

Chapter 3

1 The impact of the newspaper on Chinese public opinion in the 1870s is documented in Mary Backus Rankin, *Elite Activism and Political Transformatin in China, Zhejiang Province, 1865–1911*, Stanford: Stanford University Press, 1986, pp. 136–69.

2 For a summary of economic development in the second half of the nineteenth century, see Albert Feuerwerker, "The Chinese Economy, ca. 1870–1911", in Dennis Twitchett and John K. Fairbank, eds. *The Cambridge History of China, vol. 11, Late Ch'ing, Part 2*, etc.

3 John L. Rawlinson, *China's Struggle for Naval Development, 1839–1895*, Cambridge, MA: Harvard University Press, 1967, p. 49.

4 David Wright, "Careers in Western science in nineteenth-century China: Xu Shou and Xu Jianyin", *Journal of the Royal Asiatic Society*, 5:1, 1995, pp. 49–91.

5 A summary account of the technology is available in Craig Dietrich, "Cotton culture and manufacture in early Ch'ing China", W. E. Willmott, ed. *Economic Organization in Chinese Society*, Stanford: Stanford University Press, 1972, pp. 109–35.

6 Joseph Needham and Wang Ling, *Science and Civilization in China, vol. 4, Physics and Physical Technology, Part 2, Mechanical Invention*, Cambridge: Cambridge University Press, 1965, pp. 135–55 and 380–7 argues that elements of the steam engine might have been invented in China, but the argument does not alter the fact that the elements did not add up to a steam engine. This argument is stronger than Needham's paper under the challenging title, "The pre-natal history of the steam-engine", *Transactions of the Newcomen Society* 35, 1962–1963, pp. 3–58. For the transformation of the Chinese bellows into a series of cranks, see Li Chongzhou, "Gudai kexue faming shuili yetie gufengji 'shuipai' ji qi fuyuan", (The "water-driven panel", water-driven bellows for iron

smelting invented by ancient science and its reconstruction) *Wenwu,*
1959:5, pp. 45–48. The argument of Peter Mathias that the invention
of the steam engine was due less to the emergence of new engineering
principles than to novelty in the application of skills to existing
technologies warns against the ready conclusion that a technology was
viable when the evidence points merely to its existence in print. See
Mathias' argument on the application of the lathe in the invention of
the steam engine in his *The First Industrial Nation: An Economic History of
Britain 1700–1914,* London: Methuen, 1983, p. 127. On the importance
of Wilkinson's cannon-boring mill to James Watt's steam engine, see L.
T. C. Rolt, *Tools for the Job, A Short History of Machine Tools,* London: B. T.
Batsford Ltd., 1965, pp. 49–50, 53–54.

7   For a brief summary of the 'Self-strengthening movement", see Ting-
yee Kuo and Kwang-ching Liu, "Self-strengthening: The pursuit of
Western technology", in John K. Fairbank, ed. *The Cambridge History of
China, vol. 10, Late Ch'ing, 1800–1911, Part I,* Cambridge: Cambridge
University Press, 1978, pp. 491–542. This may be supplemented by Liu
Guangjing (Kwang-ching Liu), *Jingshi sixiang yu xinxing qiye* (Statecraft
thinking and the newly rising enterprises), Taibei: Lianjing, 1990.

8   I am indebted to Wang Hsien-chun, completing his doctoral dissertation
at Oxford, for some of the ideas in this paragraph.

9   Roger Greatrex, "Comparative perspectives upon the introduction of
Western steamship technology to Japan and China", *Senri Ethnological
Studies,* No. 46, 1998, pp. 99–126, presents the very interesting argument
that the Japanese success in steamship technology had to do with its
indigenization, while the Chinese failure might be linked to its being
thought of as a foreign technology.

10 "Medieval businessmen ... could not escape the fact that in no European
legal jurisdiction was there such a concept as 'inalienable rights': there
were only legal privileges. Because privilege in essence means 'private
law', one's legal standing depended on either the customary privileges
attached to one's status as a noble, peasant, or burher, or prerogatives
granted by charter or other agreement by a king or other sovereign
power." Edwin S. Hunt and James M. Murray, *A History of Business in
Medieval Europe, 1200–1550,* Cambridge: Cambridge University Press,
1999, p. 75.

11 A convenient summary of the use of written contracts in Chinese history
may be found in Valerie Hansen, *Negotiating Daily Life in Traditional
China: How Ordinary People Used Contracts, 600–1400,* New Haven: Yale
University Press, 1995.

12 Fu-mei Chang Chen and Ramon H. Myers, "Customary law and the
economic growth of China during the Ch'ing period", *Ch'ing-shih*

wen-t'i, 3:5, 1976, pp. 1–32; 3:10; 1978, pp. 4–27, James Hayes, "Specialists and written materials in the village world", David Johnson, Andrew J. Nathan and Evelyn S. Rawski, eds. *Popular Culture in Late Imperial China*, Berkeley: University of California Press, 1985, pp. 75–111; Myron L. Cohen, "Family partition as contractual procedure in Taiwan: A case study from south Taiwan", David C. Buxbaum, ed. *Chinese Family Law and Social Change in Historical and Comparative Perspective*, Seattle: University of Washington Press, 1978, pp. 176–204, and Rosser H. Brockman, "Commercial contract law in late nineteenth-century Taiwan", in Jerome Alan Cohen, R. Randle Edwards and Fu-mei Chang Chen, eds. *Essays on China's Legal Tradition*, Princeton: Princeton University Press, 1980, pp. 76–136.

13   Evidence from Taiwan suggests that perhaps 20 percent of the cases that appeared before the magistrate were primarily civil. This argues that the magistrate was involved in the settlement of private disputes, not that merchants would readily bring to his attention disputes in relation to trade. For relevant material on this argument, see David C. Buxbaum, "Some aspects of civil procedure and practice at the trial level in Tanshui and Hsinchu from 1789 to 1895", *Journal of Asian Studies*, 30:2, 1971, pp. 255–79. On the role of the guild, see Lu Zuoxie, "Ming-Qing shiqi de huiguan bingfei gongshangye hanghui" (The guildhalls in the Ming and Qing periods were not commercial and industrial guilds), *Zhongguoshi yanjiu*, 1982:2, pp. 66–79. Lu's comments may be supplemented by Susan Mann, *Local Merchants and the Chinese Bureaucracy 1750–1950*, Stanford: Stanford University Press, 1987, and William T. Rowe, *Hankow, Commerce and Society in a Chinese City, 1796–1889*, Stanford: Stanford University Press, 1984.

14   Zhang Haipeng and Wang Tingyuan, *Ming-Qing Huishang ziliao xuanbian*, Hefe: Huangshan shushe 1985, pp. 270–1. Compare the following contract cited by Fernand Braudel from Nantes, dated 1719: "No money will be taken out of the firm except what is necessary for the livelihood and upkeep of each partner's family, so as not to diminish its capital; and for no other purpose, and whenever one partner takes out money, he must inform the other, who will take the same amount, so that no accounts will need to be kept under this heading." See Fernand Braudel, *Civilization and Capitalism*, Vol. 2, p. 438. Braudel sees in the Nantes contract a "family or near-family atmosphere".

15   Deng Tuo 1963, "Cong Wanli dao Qianlong", *op. cit.*; Tang Mingsui, Li Longqian, Zhang Weixiong 1960, "Dui Deng Tuo tongzhi 'Cong Wanli dao Qianlong' yi wen de shangque he buchong" (A discussion of and supplement to Comrade Deng Tuo's essay, "From Wanli to Qianlong"), in Nanjing daxue lishixi Zhongguo gudaishi jiaoyanshi, ed. *Zhongguo*

ziben zhuyi mengya wenti taolun ji, Beijing, 1960, pp. 218–32; Fang Xing, "Qingdai Beijing diqu caimei ye zhong de ziben zhuyi mengya" (The sprouts of capitalism in the coal mining business in Qing period Beijing area), in *Zhongguo shehui kexueyuan jingji yanjiusuo jikan*, no. 2, 1981, pp. 186–212; Ling Yaolun, "Lun Qingdai Zigong jingyanye ziben zhuyi mengya shougongchang de fazhan" (A discussion of the sprouts of capitalism in the handicraft workshops among the salt wells of Zigong in the Qing period), in Chen Ran, Xie Qichou, Qiu Mingda, eds. *Zhongguo yanyeshi luncong*, Beijing: Zhongguo shehui chubanshe 1987, pp. 518–43; Madeleine Zelin, "Capital accumulation and investment strategies in early modern China: The case of the Furong salt yard", *Late Imperial China*, vol. 9, no. 1, 1988, pp. 79–122. For a sample of the account kept in favour of a shareholder, see Deng Tuo, "Cong Wanli dao Qianlong", pp. 222–24, and see discussion of the term *"yimei"* that appears in this document in Fang Xing, "Qingdai Beijing caimei ye", p. 196.

16   Takeda Kasuo, "Tozai juroku seiki shosan no taiketsu", (A comparison of sixteenth-century commercial arithmetic in the East and the West) in *Kagakushi kenkyu*, no. 36, 1955, pp. 17–22; no. 38, pp. 10–16; no. 39, pp. 7–14; Huang Yinpu, "Guangzhou shi guyou shangye buji zhidu zhi yanjiu" (A study of existing commercial accounting systems in Guangzhou city), *Shehui kexue luncong*, 3:5, 1931, pp. 137–56. Takeshi Hamashita, as discussant of the lecture in 1994 on which this chapter is based, pointed out that traditional Chinese business accounts were not so much designed for tracking the account balance as for the tracking of human relationships. I think there is a great deal of truth in this observation.

17   A substantial literature has appeared on the subject of the lineage trust since Maurice Freedman's seminal *Chinese Lineage and Society: Fukien and Kwangtung*, London: Athlone Press, 1966. For recent statements, see Myron L. Cohen, "Shared beliefs: Corporations, community and religion among the south Taiwan Hakka during the Ch'ing", *Late Imperial China*, 14:1, 1993, pp. 1–33; Zheng Zhenman, *Ming-Qing Fujian jiazu zuzhi yu shehui bianqian* (Lineage organization and social change in Ming-Qing Fujian), Hunan Jiaoyu, 1992, translated into English by Michael Szonyi as Zheng Zhenman, *Practicing Kinship, Lineage and Descent in Late Imperial China*, Stanford: Stanford University Press, 2002; and Kentaro Matsubara, "Law of the Ancestors: property holding practices and lineage social structures in nineteenth century south China", unpublished D.Phil. dissertation, Oxford University, 2004.

18   *Xin'an xianzhi* (The local history of Xin'an county), 1819, rep. Hong Kong, 1979, p. 83.

19 Jiang Canteng, *Wan-Ming Fojiao conglin gaige yu Foxue zhengbian zhi yanjiu — yi Hanshan Deqing de gaige shengya wei zhongxin* (The reform of the Buddhist monastic order at the end of the Ming and Buddhist theological debate — a study focused on the reforming life of Hanshan Deqing), Taipei: Xin wenfeng chubanshe, 1990, pp. 136–72.

20 Liu Zhiwei, *Zai guojia yu shehui zhi jian — Ming-Qing Guangdong lijia fuyi zhidu yanjiu* (Between state and society — a study of lijia tax and service in Ming and Qing Guangdong), Guangzhou: Zhongshan daxue chubanshe, 1997.

21 The issue of whether a corporation is or is not more than a collection of individual contracts is a question that arose in Western law but not in Chinese rituals. Chinese rituals bypass the issue by assuming that land could be held under names, some of which were ancestral. Ming and Qing administrative practice accommodated registration under names of deceased persons and so no conflict arose between the "law" and common practice, where the name pertained to a historic person, real or imaginary. For another interpretation, see Teemu Ruskola, "Conceptualizing corporations and kinship: Comparative law and development theory in a Chinese perspective", *Stanford Law Review*, 52:6, 2000, pp. 1599–729.

22 Examples are abundant in the genealogies and some are cited in *The Structure of Chinese Rural Society: Lineage and Village in the Eastern New Territories of Hong Kong*, Hong Kong: Oxford University Press, 1986. However, again ink is pointlessly spilt because writers on the subject do not distinguish the different kinds of land rights that accrued to these institutions. The heavy reliance on Maurice Freedman, *Chinese Lineage and Society: Fukien and Kwangtung*, op. cit., exaggerates the importance of land rights created by purchase or registration — the sort that led to the rotation described here — as an essential function of the lineage. Quite apart from any benefits that might be derived from such holdings, membership to the lineage might grant the right of residence and reclamation, and that would not entail the holding of any property as a "trust".

23 Zheng Zhenman, "Shenmiao jidian yu shequ fazhan moshi — Putian Jiangkou pingyuan de lizheng" (Temple sacrificial ritual and a model of regional development — the case of the Jiangkou plain in Putian), *Shilin*, 1995, pp. 275–47, 111; Huang Zhusan and Feng Junjie, eds. *Hongdong Jiexiu shuili beike jilu* (A collection of stele inscriptions on water management in Hongdong and Jiexiu), Beijing: Zhonghua, 2003.

24 Chi-cheung Choi, "Competition among brothers: The Kin Tye Lung Company and its associate companies", in Rajeswary Ampalavanar Brown, *Chinese Business Enterprise* vol. 1, pp. 65–82, and "Kinship and

business: paternal and maternal kin in Chaozhou Chinese family firms",
Business History, 40:1, 1998, pp. 26–49.

25   For another example, see Zhongguo kexue yuan jingji yanjiusuo,
Zhongyang gongshang xingzheng guanliju, ziben zhuyi jingji gaizuo
yanjiushi, eds. *Beijing Ruifuxiang* (The Ruifuxiang of Beijing), Beijing,
1959. The experience of the Meng family in north China cities, including
Beijing, is also discussed in Wellington K. K. Chan, "The Organizational
Structure of the Traditional Chinese Firm and Its Modern Reform",
Business History Review, 1982, pp. 218–35. In the 1920s and 1930s, this
very traditional method of corporate control was employed in the
business of the Shanghai businessman, Liu Hongsheng, who advocated
scientific management. On Liu Hongsheng, see Kai-yiu Chan, "The
structure of Chinese business in republican China: The case of Liu
Hongsheng and his enterprises, 1920–1937", unpublished D.Phil. thesis,
University of Oxford, 1997.

26   Ian Inkster, "Pursuing big books: Technological change in global
history", in Graham Hollister-Short, ed. *History of Technology, vol. 22*,
London: Continuum, 2001, pp. 233–53.

Chapter 4

1   What I refer to in this chapter as government enterprises were
enterprises managed on the "official supervision, merchant
management" model.

2   For studies of some of these firms in English, see Albert Feuerwerker,
China's Early Industrialization; Sherman Cochran, *Big Business in China*;
and Elisabeth Koll, *From Cotton Mill to Business Empire.*

3   For the use of the term "*gongsi*" as a translation of the East India
Company, see E. C. Bridgman, *Chinese Chrestomathy in the Canton Dialect*,
Macao: S. Wells Williams, 1841, p. 234; and Ernest John Eitel, *A Chinese
Dictionary of the Cantonese Dialect*, London: Trubner and Co., 1877, p. 305.
Compare the more general use of the term in A. Dyer Ball, *Cantonese
Made Easy*, Shanghai: Kelly and Walsh, 1889, p. 126; and George Carter
Stent, *Chinese and English Vocabulary in the Pekinese Dialect*, Shanghai:
American Presbyterian Mission Press, 1898, p. 346. Stent translates
"*gongsi*" as "to manage public business, a public company". For the
Southeast Asian context, see Wang Tai Peng, *The Origins of Chinese Kongsi*,
Selangor Darul Ehsan, Malaysia: Pelanduk Publications (M) Sdn Bhd,
1994; and for a reference in which this term was used in 1683, see
Matsuura Sho, "Qingdai '*gongsi*' xiaokao" (A short study of the "*gongsi*"
in the Qing), transl. by Hua Li, in *Qingshi yanjiu*, vol. 10, 1993, pp. 95–
98. I am grateful to Dr Hon Honwai for drawing my attention to some
of these references.

4 The suggestions to nationalize China Merchants' Steam Navigation Co. from 1878 to 1881 are relevant here. See Chi-kong Lai, "Lunchuan zhaoshang chu guoyou wenti, 1878–1881" (The proposal to nationalize the China Merchants' Steam Navigation Co., 1878–1881", *Bulletin of the Institute of Modern History, Academia Sinica*, vol. 17, 1988, pp. 15–40.

5 Bishop Carleton Hunt, *The Development of the Business Corporation in England 1800–1867*, Cambridge, MA: Harvard University Press, 1936.

6 Zhang Guohui, *Yangwu yundong yu Zhongguo jindai qiye* (The Self-strengthening Movement and Chinese modern enterprise), Beijing: Zhongguo shehui keshe, 1979, pp. 129–34.

7 For brief documentation of these complicated events, see Liu Jinzao, ed. *Huangchao xu wenxian tongkao* (Supplementary general survey of documents of the imperial dynasty), n.p., 1921, 361/1.

8 A very useful brief summary of "official supervision and merchant management" may be found in Shao Xunzheng, "Guanyu yangwu pai minyong qiye de xingzhi he daolu — lun guandu shangban" (On the nature and direction of the pro-Western faction's civilian enterprise — a discussion of official supervision and merchant management), *Xin jianshe*, 1964:1, reprinted in Shao Xunzheng, *Shao Xunzheng lishi lunwenji*, Beijing: Beijing daxue, 1985, pp. 349–71.

9 Albert Feuerwerker, *China's Early Industrialization*, pp. 124–49, the quote being taken from p. 127.

10 Wang Jingyu, "Shijiu shiji waiguo qinhua qiye zhong de huashang fugu huodong" (Share-affiliation by Chinese merchants in foreign enterprises detrimental to China in the nineteenth century), *Lishi yanjiu* 1965:4, reprinted in Huang Yiping, ed. *Zhongguo jindai jingjishi lunwen xuan*, Shanghai: Shanghai renmin, 1985, pp. 193–257.

11 K. C. Liu, *Anglo-American Steamship Rivalry in China 1862–1874*, Cambridge, MA: Harvard University Press, 1962, p. 184 n. 67.

12 E. J. Eitel, *Europe in China*, Hong Kong: Oxford University Press, 1983 reprint of 1895 edition; pp. 367–8. On the legality of companies registered in Hong Kong trading in China, see W. A. Thomas, *Western Capitalism in Chin: A History of the Shanghai Stock Exchange*, Aldershot: Ashgate, 2001, pp. 28–32.

13 Wang Jingyu, "Shijiu shiji waiguo qinhua qiye zhong de huashang fugu huodong", p. 206, also makes the point that ship registration in Shanghai from 1875 facilitated Chinese investment in shipping, and he cites *Consular Reports* Shanghai, 1880, p. 101, for a corroborating contemporary opinion.

14 Frank H. H. King, *The History of the Hongkong and Shanghai Banking Corporation*, Cambridge: Cambridge University Press, vol. 1, pp. 61–62.

15 When Augustine Heard advertised for share capital in favour of his

shipping company in 1862, he failed to raise any in Shanghai. When Jing Yuanshan did the same for the cotton cloth mill in 1880, it was over-subscribed. For Heard's attempt, see Wang Jingyu, "Shijiu shiji waiguo qinhua qiye zhong de huashang fugu huodong", p. 197, for Jing Yuanshan, see Zhang Guohui, *Yangwu yundong yu Zhongguo jindai qiye*, p. 368.

16   Zhang Guohui, *Yangwu yundong yu Zhongguo jindai qiye*, p. 369.

17   Hong Jiaguan, Zhang Jifeng, *Jindai Shanghai jinrong shichang*, Shanghai: Shanghai renmin, 1989, pp. 134–8, 145–9. See also an article in support of stock-broking from the *Shenbao* of 27 September 1882 cited on p. 145; W. A. Thomas, *Western Capitalism in China*, pp. 93–117, finds that share dealings appeared in the 1860s but the Shanghai Stock and Sharebrokers' Association was formed in 1898.

18   Yen-ping Hao, *The Compradore in Nineteenth Century China: Bridge Between East and West*, Cambridge: East Asian Research Centre, Harvard University, 1970, p. 100.

19   Chen Shiqi, "Sheng Xuanhuai de ziben ji qi longduan huodong" (Sheng Xuanhuai's capital and his monopolistic activities), *Xiamen daxue xuebao (shehui kexue ban)*, 1962:3, pp. 1–22; Beijing daxue lishixi jindaishi jiaoyanshi, *Sheng Xuanhuai weikan xingao* (Sheng Xuanhuai's unpublished letters), Beijing: Xinhua shudian, 1960, pp. 268–87.

20   Albert Feuerwerker, *China's Early Industrialization*, pp. 146–7; Zhang Guohui, *Yangwu yundong yu Zhongguo jindai qiye*, pp. 360–1.

21   Shao Xunzheng, "Yangwu yundong he Zhongguo zichan jieji fazhan de guanxi wenti" (The question of the relationship between the Self-strengthening Movement and the development of the capitalist class in China), *Xin jianshe*, 1963:3, reprinted in Shao Xunzheng, *Shao Xunzheng lishi lunwenji*, pp. 301–22; Wang Jingyu, "Cong Shanghai qiqi zhipuchu kan yangwu yundong he ziben zhuyi fazhan guanxi wenti" (The question of the development of the relationship between the Self-strengthening Movement and capitalism as seen from the Shanghai Cotton Cloth Mill), *Xin jianshe*, 1963, no. 8, pp. 35–44; Albert Feuerwerker, *China's Early Industrialization*, pp. 207–25; and Edward Le Fevour, *Western Enterprise in Late Ch'ing China: A Selective Survey of Jardine, Matheson & Company's Operations, 1842–1895*, Cambridge, MA: East Asian Research Centre, Harvard University, 1970, pp. 40–47.

22   Quan Hansheng, *Hanyeping gongsi shilue* (A brief history of the Hanyeping Co.), Hong Kong: Chinese University Press, 1972.

23   He Hanwei, "Cong yinjian qianhuang dao tongyuan fanlan — Qingmo xin huobi de faxing ji qi yingxiang" (From the devaluing of silver and the scarcity of copper cash to the oversupply of the copper coinage — the issuing of new currency in the late Qing and its effects), *Zhongyang yanjiuyuan lishi yuyan yanjiusuo jikan* 62:3, 1993, pp. 389–494.

24 Lillian M. Li, *China's Silk Trade: Traditional Industry in the Modern World, 1842–1937*, Cambridge, MA: Council on East Asian Studies, Harvard University, 1981; Robert Eng, *Economic Imperialism in China: Silk Production and Exports, 1861–1932*, Berkeley: Institute of East Asian Studies, University of California, 1986.

25 Shanghai shi gongshang xingzheng guanliju, Shanghai shi diyi jidian gongyeju, jiqi gongye shiliao zu, eds. *Shanghai minzu jiqi gonye* (The Shanghai native machinery industry), Beijing: Zhonghua, 1979 rep. (first ed. 1966), pp. 74–88.

26 Ibid., p. 111.

27 Compiled from Du Xuncheng, *Minzu ziben zhuyi yu jiu Zhongguo zhengfu (1840–1937)* (Native capitalism and the old Chinese government, 1840–1937), Shanghai: Shanghai shehui kexueyuan, 1991, pp. 285–528. See also Michael Godley, *The Mandarin-Capitalists from Nanyang: Overseas Chinese Enterprise in the Modernization of China, 1893–1911*, Cambridge: Cambridge University Press, 1981.

28 Qian Jiaqu, "Jiu Zhongguo fahang gongzhai shi de yanjiu" (A study of public debt issued in old China), *Lishi yanjiu* 1955: 2, rep. in Cuncui xueshe, *Zhongguo jin sanbai nian*, vol. 5, pp. 12–13.

29 Wang Ermin, "Shangzhan guannian yu zhongshang sixiang" (The concept of commercial war and the mercantilist ideology", in Wang Ermin, *Zhongguo jindai sixiang shilun*, Taipei, published by the author, 1977, pp. 233–379. According to Wang, the idea of commercial war originated with Zeng Guofan in 1860 but became popular from the late 1880s.

30 Wang Jingyu, *Zhongguo jindai gongyeshi ziliao, di'erji, 1895–1914* (Materials on modern Chinese industrial history, part 2, 1895–1914), Beijing: Kexue, 1957, p. 580.

31 Sun Yutang, *Zhongguo jindai gongyeshi ziliao, diyiji, 1895–1914* (Materials on modern Chinese industrial history, part 1, 1840–1895), Beijing: Kexue, 1957, pp. 709–10.

32 Wang Jingyu, *Zhongguo jindai gongyeshe ziliao*, p. 683.

33 Wang Jingyu, *Zhongguo jindai gongyeshe ziliao*, p. 635.

34 Dasheng xitong qiye shi bianxiezu, *Dasheng xitong qiye* (The enterprise of the Dasheng system), Jiangsu guji, 1990, pp. 10–17.

35 Lee En-han, *China's Quest for Railway Autonomy 1904–1911, A Study of the Chinese Railway-Rights Recovery Movement*, Singapore: Singapore University Press, 1977, pp. 96–98.

36 Quan Hansheng, "Qingji tielu jianshe de ziben wenti" (The question of capital in the building of railways in the Qing), in Quan Hansheng, *Zhongguo jingjishi yanjiu*, Hong Kong: Xinya yanjiusuo, 1976, pp. 229–52.

37 Wellington K. K. Chan, *Merchants, Mandarins and Modern Enterprise in Late Ch'ing China*, Cambridge, MA: East Asian Research Centre, Harvard University, 1977, p. 153.

38 George Jamieson, *Chinese Family and Commercial Law*, Shanghai: Kelly and Walsh, 1921, p. i.

39 G. W. Keeton, *The Development of Extraterritoriality in China*, New York: Howard Fertig, 1969, vol. 2, p. 373.

40 G. W. Keeton, *The Development of Extraterritoriality*, p. 365.

41 *North China Herald*, supplement, 10 September 1902, and George Jamieson, *Chinese Family and Commercial Law*, pp. 178–9.

42 Barely nine months elapsed between the appointment of Wu Tingfang and others in April 1903 and their presentation of the completed draft bills in January 1904. See *Guangxu chao donghua lu* (A record of the Guangxu reign), Beijing: Zhonghua, 1958, pp. 5013–4 and p. 5132. An article by George Jamieson on British company law might have served as the model. See Zhemeisen, "Yingguo gongsi dingli" (Regulations on companies in England), Chen Zhongyi, ed. *Huangchao jingshiwen sanbian* (State craft essays of the dynasty, third compilation, n.p., preface of 1898), 39/3b–5b.

43 George Jamieson, *Chinese Family and Commercial Law*, pp. 124–5.

44 Xu Dingxin, Qian Xiaoming, *Shanghai zhong shanghui shi (1902–1929)* (A history of the Shanghai General Chamber of Commerce, 1902–1929), Shanghai: Shanghai shehui kexueyuan, 1991, pp. 94–96.

45 Chen Zhen, Yao Luo, eds. *Zhongguo jindai gongyeshi ziliao* (Sources on the history of modern Chinese industry), Beijing: Sanlian, 1957, vol. 1, p. 10, shows that up to 1920 only 1,167 companies and 475 factories had registered with the Chinese government; William C. Kirby, "China unincorporated: Company law and business enterprise in twentieth-century China", *Journal of Asian Studies* 24.1, 1995, pp. 43–63.

Chapter 5

1 I am not so much thinking of the economic theories implied by the concept of marginal utility as the close correspondence between Menger's and Weber's view of social theory, which is well brought out in F. A. Hayek, "Carl Menger (1840–1921)", in F. A. Hayek, *The Collected Works of F. A. Hayek*, ed. by Seton G. Klein, London: Routledge, 1992, vol. 4, pp. 61–107. See in particular p. 102 and the editor's note on p. 78.

2 Lynn T. White III, *Policies of Chaos: The Organizational Causes of Violence in China's Cultural Revolution*, Princeton: Princeton University Press, 1989.

3 Audrey Donnithorne, "China's cellular economy: Some economic trends since the Cultural Revolution", *China Quarterly* 52, 1972, pp. 605–19.

4 A. G. Walder, *Communist Neo-Traditionalism: Work and Authority in Chinese Industry*, Berkeley: University of California Press, 1986.

5 Jean C. Oi, *State and Peasant in Contemporary China: The Political Economy of Village Government*, Berkeley: University of California Press, 1989.

6 Hong-yung Lee, *From Revolutionary Cadres to Party Technocrats in Socialist China*, Berkeley: University of California Press, 1991, p. 208.

7 Carl Riskin, "Neither plan nor market: Mao's political economy", William A. Joseph, Christine P. W. Wong and David Zweig, eds. *New Perspectives on the Cultural Revolution*, Cambridge, MA: Council on East Asian Studies, Harvard University, 1991, p. 140.

8 Nicholas R. Lardy, "Economic development in the PRC", in Ramon H. Myers, ed. *Two Societies in Opposition: The Republic of China and the People's Republic of China after Forty Years*, Stanford: Hoover Institution Press, 1991, pp. 180–97.

9 Helen F. Siu, *Agents and Victims in South China: Accomplices in Rural Revolution*, New Haven: Yale University Press, 1989, p. 292.

10 China's foreign trade doubled between 1972 and 1974, and doubled again between 1977 and 1979. See Nicholas R. Lardy, *Foreign Trade and Economic Reform in China, 1978–1990*, Cambridge: Cambridge University Press, 1992, p. 12.

11 Yang Liansheng, *Zhongguo wenhua zhong "bao", "bao", "bao" zhi yiyi* (The meaning of the characters "bao", "bao" and "bao" in Chinese culture), Hong Kong: Chinese University Press, 1987. The three characters may be translated as "retribution", "patronage", and "contract" and should be considered central to any study of the historical economy.

12 Du Runsheng, "Woguo nongye jitihua de guoqu yu xianzai" (The past and present of agricultural collectivization in our country), talk given on 28 November 1980, reprinted in Du Runsheng, *Zhongguo nongcun jingji gaige*, Beijing: Zhongguo shehui kexue, 1985, pp. 10–25.

13 Wang Jiye and Zhu Yuanzhen, comps. *Jingji tizhi gaige shouce* (Handbook of economic structural reforms), Beijing: Jingji ribao, 1987, pp. 73–76.

14 Wang Jiye and Zhu Yuanzhen, comps. *Jingji tizhi gaige shouce*, p. 86.

15 Tang Tsou, *The Cultural Revolution and Post-Mao Reforms, A Historical Perspective*, Chicago: University of Chicago Press, 1986, pp. 194–5.

16 Helen F. Siu, *Agents and Victims*, pp. 274–7.

17 Sulamith Heins Potter and Jack M. Potter, *China's Peasant: The Anthropology of a Revolution*, Cambridge: Cambridge University Press, 1990, p. 173.

18 Victor Nee, "Peasant entrepreneurship and the politics of regulation in China", in Victor Nee and David Stark, eds. *Remaking the Economic Institutions of Socialism: China and East Europe*, Stanford: Stanford University Press, 1989, pp. 184–5.

19   F. W. Crook, "The *baogan-daohu* incentive system — translation and analysis of a model-contract", *China Quarterly* 102, 1985, pp. 291–303; and Sulamith Heins Potter and Jack M. Potter, *China's Peasants*, pp. 173–4.

20   Zhonghua renmin gongheguo nongyebu jihuasi, *Zhongguo nongcun jingji tongji daquan, 1949–1986* (The complete statistics on China's rural economy, 1949–1986), Beijing: Nongye, 1989, p. 434.

21   The most comprehensive of these policy statements was "Guomuyuan guanyu nongcun geti gongshangye de ruogan guiding" (Certain State Council regulations concerning rural individual-household industry and commerce), 27 February 1984, which may be found in Wang Jiye and Zhu Yuanzhen, comps. *Jingji tizhi gaige shouce*, pp. 233–5.

22   Guojia tongjiju nongcun shehui jingji tongjisi, comp. *Zhongguo nongcun tongji nianjian, 1987* (Yearbook of the rural statistics of China, 1987), Beijing: Zhongguo tongji, 1987, p. 12.

23   Zhang Musheng and Bai Ruobing, "Guanyu dangqian nongcun 'gugong' jingying de shijian yu lilun" (On the practice and theory of present 'hired labour' management in agricultural villages), Zhongguo nongcun fazhan wenti yanjiuzu, ed., *Nongcun, jingji, shehui*, vol. 3, Beijing: zhishi, 1985, pp. 172 and 173.

24   Bai Nansheng, Xu Kuan and Zhao Mingyu, " 'Shuangbao dao hu" hou de laodongli he zijin biandong quxi — Anhui sheng Chuxian diqu nongcun diaocha zhuanti baogao" (Trends in labour force and capital after "Double-responsibilities to the household" — special report on an investigation in villages of the Chuxian area of Anhui province), in Zhongguo nongcun fazhan wenti yanjiuzu, ed., *Nongcun, jingji, shehui*, vol. 1, Beijing: zhishi, 1985, p.141; Zhang Musheng, "Nongcun minban daxing lianheti he chengbao dahu tansuo — Guangxi Wuzhou diqu yu Guangdong Gaoyao xian diaocha" (Investigation into rural private large-scale cooperative body and big households in responsibility contracts — an investigation of Wuzhou region in Guangxi and Gaoyao xian in Guangdong), in Zhongguo nongcun fazhan wenti yanjiuzu, ed., *Nongcun, jingji, shehui*, vol. 2, Beijing: zhishi, 1985, p. 91.

25   Gao Kuanzhong, "Woguo chengbao nonghu falu diwei chutan" (A first investigation into the legal status of rural households in our country), in Tong Rou, ed. *Jingji tizhi gaige zhong de ruogan minfa wenti*, Beijing: Beijing shifan xueyuan, 1985, pp. 128–46.

26   Qian Hang and Xie Weiyang, "Qinzu juju xianxiang yu woguo dangqian nongcun de zongzu huodong" (The phenomenon of common settlement among relatives and current rural lineage activities in our country), *Xueshu jikan* 1991:3, pp. 162–3.

27   Wang Huning, *Dangdai Zhongguo cunluo jiazu wenhua — dui Zhongguo xiandaihua de yixiang tansuo* (Village and family culture in contemporary China — an investigation into China's modernization), Shanghai: Shanghai renmin, 1991.

28   In his address to the National Agricultural Conference in December 1984, Wan Li noted, "(Some people) only consider the original village (*xiang* and *cun*) and brigade collective enterprises as township and village enterprises. They do not include as township and village enterprises those enterprises founded individually or through the raising of capital by the peasants as a group. Some of them even despise such enterprises. This is not correct. In actual fact, in many places, the enterprises founded individually or through the raising of capital by the peasants as a group are a very important part of future township and village enterprise development. Their production amounts to over half of all production from township and village enterprises. Therefore, they should be regarded as equal, and given encouragement and support." *Hongqi* 1985, no. 2, reprinted in Shen Chong, Xiang Xiyang, *Shinian lai: lilun, zhengce, shijian — ziliao xuanbian* (The past ten years: Theory, policy and practice — selection of source materials), Beijing: Qiushi, 1988, vol. 2, p. 364.

29   "Guanyu woguo geti jingji de fazhan zhuangkuang he quanzhai de zhuyao wenti" (Major questions concerning the development and survival of the private economy of our country), *Jingji tizhi gaike neibu cankao* 1987, no. 22, reprinted in Shen Chong, Xiang Xiyang, *Shinian lai*, vol. 3, p. 351.

30   Zheng Dajiong, *Wenzhou gaige — lilun sikao yu shijian tansuo* (Reforms in Wenzhou — a search in theoretical thinking and practice), Shanghai: Fudan daxue, 1991.

31   Tao Youzhi, *Sunan moshi yu zhifu zhidao* (The southern Jiangsu model and the road to wealth), Shanghai: Shanghai shehui kexue, 1988, pp. 103–8.

32   Fei Xiaotong, "Xiao chengzhen, da wenti" (Small towns, big problems), talk given in 1983, reprinted in Fei Xiaotong, *Xiao chengzhen siji*, Beijing: Xinhua, 1985, pp. 1–50.

33   *Guangming ribao*, 1 December 1986, p. 1.

34   Huang Rong, Chen Daojin, "Gai sheban wei hegu lianban, zengqiang liao qiye huoli" (Transforming commune management to share management, strengthening enterprise liveliness), in *Su, Zhe, Yue xiangzhen qiye chenggong zhi lu*, Guangzhou: Guangdong renmin, 1985, pp. 245–7.

35   Shen Chong, Xiang Xiyang, *Shinian lai*, p. 401, citing *Renmin ribao* (People's Daily), 13 December 1983.

36 Cao Pei and Ni Zhengmao, "Nongcun shangpin jingji fazhan zhong biqie xuyao jiejue de jige falu wenti ji qiyou jianyi — fu Shandong Yantai diqu Jiling xian de diaocha baogao" (Several questions of law that urgently need to be solved and related proposals in the development of the rural commercial economy — report of an investigation from a visit to Jiling xian in the Yantai area in Shandong), in Tong Rou, ed. *Jingji tizhi gaige zhong de ruogan minfa wenti*, pp. 147–67, quotation from p. 155.

37 Cyril Zhiren Lin, "Open-ended economic reform in China", in Victor Nee and David Stark, *Remaking the Economic Institutions of Socialis*, p. 113.

38 William A. Byrd, "Contractual responsibility systems in Chinese state-owned industry: A preliminary assessment", in Nigel Campbell, Sylvian R. F. Plasechaert and David H. Brown, eds. *Advances in Chinese Industrial Studies, Vol. 2, The Changing Nature of Management in China*, Greenwich, CT: Jai Press Inc., 1991, pp. 7–35.

39 Berhanu Abegaz and Clyde A. Haulman, "The economic implications of enterprise financial autonomy in China", in John Child and Martin Lockett, eds. *Advances in Chinese Industrial Studies, vol. 1, pt. A, Reform Policy and the Chinese Enterprise*, Greenwich, CT: Jai Press, 1990, p. 52.

40 Liu Siwei, "Guanyu qingli zhengdun gongsi de sikao" (Some thoughts on streamlining and reorganizing companies), *Guangming ribao*, 13 January 1990.

41 William A. Byrd, "The Second Motor Vehicle Manufacturing Plant", in William A. Byrd, ed. *Chinese Industrial Firms under Reform*, Oxford: Oxford University Press, 1992, pp. 371–426. The quotation is cited from p. 411.

42 "Guomuyuan guanyu jinyibu kuoda guoying gongye qiye zizhuquan de zanxing guiding" (Temporary State Council regulations concerning the further expansion of industrial enterprise autonomy), para. 10, in Wang Jiye and Zhu Yuanzhen, comps. *Jingji tizhi gaige shouce*, p. 175.

43 Shen Chong, Xiang Xiyang, *Shinian lai*, p. 401, citing *Renmin ribao*, 27 November 1987.

44 *Renmin ribao*, 22 August 1986.

45 *Renmin ribao*, 5 April 1987, p. 1.

46 Tong Dalin, "Gufen hua shi shehui zhuyi qiye de yige xin jidian" (Shareholding is a new base point for socialist enterprise), *Renmin ribao*, 18 August 1986, p. 5; Li Yining, "Woguo suoyouzhi gaige de shexiang" (A plan for the reform of ownership systems in our country), *Renmin ribao*, 26 Septempter 1986, p. 5.

47 *South China Morning Post*, 22 March 1994.

48 *South China Morning Post*, 21 March 1994.

49 *South China Morning Post*, 23 March 1994.

50 I have found very useful the following accounts on recent developments

in accounting in China: Xie Rong, Li Shuhua and Wang Jianchun, *Zhongguo zhuce kuijishi zhiye fazhan zhanlue* (A strategy for the development of the registered accountants' profession in China), Shanghai: Lixin kuiji chubanshe, 2000; and Chen Xinyuan and Jin Nan, *Xin Zhongguo kuiji sixiang shi* (An intellectual history of new accounting in China), Shanghai: Shanghai caijing daxue chubanshe, 1999.

51 From the website of the Chinese Institute of Certified Public Accountants (http://www.cicpa.org.cn/vocation/vocation.htm), downloaded on 28 May 2004. For comparison, of the 335,000 members of the American Institute of Certified Public Accountants, 128,000 are in public practice, and the Institute of Chartered Accountants of England and Wales 125,000 members.

52 M. W. Luke Chan, "Management education in the People's Republic of China", in David H. Brown and Robin Porter, eds. *Management Issues in China*, vol. 1, London: Routledge, 1996, p. 241.

53 It would seem to me that to take this argument to its conclusion, it has to be said that in the West, especially in the United Kingdom, pension funds tend to fail miserably on any test of accountability to clients. The lesson to be drawn is not that accountability is unimportant, but that China should not blindly follow the West in its market reforms.

A Note on Further Reading for the Non-Chinese Reader

Most non-specialist readers will probably need at hand a textbook on Chinese history from the Ming dynasty onwards in order to wade through the literature. A readable account would be, for the dynastic period, Jacques Gernet, *A History of Chinese Civilization*, Cambridge: Cambridge University Press, 1982, or, for the twentieth century, Jonathan D. Spence, *The Search for Modern China*, New York: Norton, 1990. For insights into the workings of imperial government administration, read Ray Huang, *1587, a Year of No Significance: The Ming Dynasty in Decline*, New Haven: Yale University Press, 1981, or Philip A. Kuhn, *Soulstealers: The Chinese Sorcery Scare of 1768*, Cambridge, MA: Harvard University Press, 1990. For a general background volume, read R. Bin Wong, *China Transformed, Historical Change and the Limits of European Experience*, Ithaca: Cornell University Press, 1997; or one which deals specifically with the economy in the first half of the twentieth century, Thomas G. Rawski, *Economic Growth in Prewar China*, Berkeley: University of California Press, 1989.

For a focus on business, the obvious place to start for readings in English is Rajeswary Ampalavanar Brown, ed. *Chinese Business Enterprise*, London: Routledge, 1996, in four volumes. The essays included span several decades of research. Although numerous collections of Chinese articles on similar subjects exist, none has been translated into English. Where I know that a Chinese article I cite has been translated into English, I cite the translation along with the original. For other examples, read Tim Wright, ed. *The Chinese Economy in the Early Twentieth Century: Recent Chinese Studies*, New York: St. Martin's Press, 1992; Rajeswary Ampalavanar Brown, *Chinese Business Enterprise in Asia*, London: Routledge, 1995; and Xu Dixin and Wu Chengming, eds. *Chinese Capitalism, 1522–1840*, Basingstoke: Macmillan, 2000, which is the first of three volumes the two compilers produced in Chinese on the subject of the development of capitalism in China. Few Japanese articles are available in English translation. A handful on subjects relevant to this volume may be found in Linda Grove and Christian Daniels, eds. *State and Society in China: Japanese Perspectives on Ming-Qing Social and Economic History*, Tokyo: University of Tokyo Press, 1984 and the *Memoirs of the Research Department of the Toyo Bunko*, Tokyo: The Toyo Bunko, annual.

A substantial number of monographs in English deal with individual firms and businesses in China. There is as yet no substitute for Albert Feuerwerker, *China's Early Industrialization, Sheng Hsuan-huai (1844–1916) and Mandarin Enterprise*, Cambridge, MA: Harvard University Press, 1958, for the important contribution of the China Merchants Steam Navigation Company to changes in business practices in the late nineteenth century. For the reader who does not read Chinese, H. D. Fong, *Cotton Industry and Trade in China*, Tianjing: The Chihli Press, 1932, is still one of the most ready sources into the development of Chinese manufacturing before the Second World War. This book may be supplemented by H. D. Fong, *Reminiscences of a Chinese Economist at 70*, Singapore: South Seas Society, for a taste of the life of the returned Western-trained economist in China during the 1920s and 1930s. Other works of individual Chinese firms or businesses in English include: Sherman Cochran, *Big Business in China: Sino-foreign Rivalry in the Cigarette Industry, 1890–1930*, Cambridge, MA: Harvard University Press, 1990, and *Encountering Chinese Networks: Western, Japanese, and Chinese Corporations in China, 1880–1937*, Berkeley: University of California Press, 2000; Elisabeth Köll, *From Cotton Mill to Business Empire: The Emergence of Regional Enterprises in Modern China*, Cambridge, MA: Harvard University Press, 2004; and Kai-yiu Chan, *The Structure of Chinese Business in Republican China: The Case of Liu Hongsheng and His Enterprises, 1920–1937*, Hong Kong: Hong Kong University Press, forthcoming. Lillian M. Li, *China's Silk Trade: Traditional Industry in the Modern World, 1842–1937*, Cambridge, MA: Council on East Asian Studies, Harvard University, 1981, provides a simple account of China's major export industry from the mid-nineteenth to the mid-twentieth century, and Tim Wright, *Coal Mining in China's Economy and Society, 1895–1937*, Cambridge: Cambridge University Press, 1984, does the same for a major mining activity. W. A. Thomas, *Western Capitalism in China: A History of the Shanghai Stock Exchange*, Aldershot: Ashgate, 2001, gives a brief and straightforward account of the introduction of share trading into China towards the end of the nineteenth century.

Writings in English on banking and finance have been uneven. Ray Ovid Hall, *The Chinese National Banks*, Berlin, 1921, provides a succinct account of the Bank of China crisis in 1916 and, from that, insight into banking in the Republican era. Brett Sheehan, *Trust in Troubled Times: Money, Banks, and State-Society Relations in Tianjin*, Cambridge, MA: Harvard University Press, 2003, brings the subject up to date. Andrea Lee McElderry, *Shanghai Old-Style Banks (ch'ien-chuang), 1800–1935: A Traditional Institution in a Changing Society*, Ann Arbor: Center for Chinese Studies, University of Michigan, 1976, is the most ready reference on traditional banking up to the 1930s. Frank H. H. King, *The History of the Hongkong and Shanghai Banking Corporation*, Cambridge: Cambridge University Press, 1987–1991, in four substantial volumes, is a mine of interesting information even though it does not deal directly with Chinese business or banks.

On other aspects of business practices, Madeleine Zelin, Jonathan K. Ocko and Robert Gardella, eds. *Contract and Property in Early Modern China*, Stanford: Stanford University Press, 2004, is a useful addition to the literature. For background, this book should be read with Valerie Hansen, *Negotiating Daily Life in Traditional China: How Ordinary People Used Contracts, 600–1400*, New Haven: Yale University Press, 1995, and John R. Watt, *The District Magistrate in Late imperial China*, New York: Columbia University Press, 1972. For a translation of the Qing law code, see William C. Jones, transl. *The Great Qing Code*, Oxford: Clarendon Press, 1994. The introduction of Western commercial law is not as well documented by recent English studies as one might expect. For an introduction and critique, see William C. Kirby, "China unincorporated: Company law and business enterprise in twentieth-century China", *Journal of Asian Studies* 24.1, 1995, pp. 43–63.

In recent years, an abundance of monographs has appeared on the post-1949 economy. One of the best overviews of the evolution of the Chinese work environment within this period may still be had by reading the following in succession: Barry M. Richman, *Industrial Society in Communist China: A Firsthand Study of Chinese Economic Development and Management — with Significant Comparisons with Industry in India, the U.S.S.R., Japan and the United States,* New York: Random House, 1969; Stephen Andors, *China's Industrial Revolution: Politics, Planning and Management, 1949 to the Present,* New York: Pantheon, 1977; and Andrew G. Walder, *Communist Neo-Traditionalism: Work and Authority in Chinese Industry,* Berkeley: University of California Press, 1986. On changes since 1978, see Harry Harding, *China's Second Revolution: Reform After Mao,* Washington, DC: The Brookings Institution, 1987; Kenneth Lieberthal and Michel Oksenberg, *Policy Making in China: Leaders, Structures, and Processes,* Princeton: Princeton University Press, 1988; and Joseph Fewsmith, *Dilemmas of Reform in China: Political Conflict and Economic Debate,* Armonk: M.E. Sharpe, 1994. More specifically on issues of management during enterprise reforms, see William A. Byrd, ed. *Chinese Industrial Firms under Reform,* Oxford: Oxford University Press, 1992; David H. Brown and Robin Porter, eds. *Management issues in China, Vol. 1: Domestic Enterprises,* London: Routledge, 1996; and John Child and Yuan Lu, *Management issues in China, Vol. 2: International Enterprises,* London: Routledge, 1996.

Index